Density by Design

New Directions in Residential Development

Second Edition

Steven Fader

Foreword by Vincent Scully

About ULI–the Urban Land Institute

ULI–the Urban Land Institute is a nonprofit education and research institute that is supported and directed by its members. Its mission is to provide responsible leadership in the use of land in order to enhance the total environment.

ULI sponsors education programs and forums to encourage an open international exchange of ideas and sharing of experiences; initiates research that anticipates emerging land use trends and issues and proposes creative solutions based on that research; provides advisory services; and publishes a wide variety of materials to disseminate information on land use and development. Established in 1936, the Institute today has more than 15,000 members and associates from more than 50 countries representing the entire spectrum of the land use and development disciplines.

Richard M. Rosan
President

Recommended bibliographic listing

Fader, Steven. *Density by Design: New Directions in Residential Development*, Second Edition. Washington, D.C.: ULI–the Urban Land Institute, 2000.

ULI Catalog Number: N25

International Standard Book Number: 0-87420-833-5

Library of Congress Catalog Card Number: 00-100593

1025 Thomas Jefferson Street, N.W.
Suite 500 West
Washington, D.C. 20007-5201

Second Printing, 2001
Third Printing, 2002

Cover photo

Looney Ricks Kiss Architects, Inc.

ULI Project Staff

Rachelle L. Levitt
Senior Vice President, Policy and Practice
Publisher

Gayle Berens
Vice President, Real Estate Development Practice

Adrienne Schmitz
Senior Associate
Project Director

Nancy H. Stewart
Director, Book Program
Managing Editor

Nancy H. Stewart
Cherrill A. Anson
Manuscript Editors

Betsy VanBuskirk
Art Director

Fathom Creative
Layout and Design

Meg Batdorff
Cover Design

Diann Stanley-Austin
Associate Director of Publishing Operations

Karrie Underwood
Word Processor

about the author

Steven Fader

As principal of the firm Steven Fader Architect in Los Angeles, Steven Fader AIA has more than 20 years of experience in planning and architecture, for both public and private sector clients. His projects have ranged from residential new construction to adaptive use of historic structures to large-scale site and master planning. Fader holds a master of architecture degree from the University of California at Los Angeles as well as a master of urban planning degree from Cornell University. He has been a contributing author to numerous ULI publications, including *Urban Parks and Open Space*; *Value By Design: Landscape, Site Planning, and Amenities*; *Developing Urban Entertainment Centers*; and *Business and Industrial Park Development Handbook.*

acknowledgments

Many individuals have contributed to this second edition of *Density By Design*. I would like to thank the many architects and developers around the country who shared their work with me as I attempted to survey the state of the art of residential design for this book. There were many excellent projects that could not be included because of the space limitations of this one small volume.

As for the projects that have been included, my particular appreciation goes to the designers, developers, sponsors, and public agencies associated with each case study project, who generously gave their time to this effort, and who, in many cases, prepared graphics especially for this book. I would also like to acknowledge those who reviewed parts of the manuscript, including Katherine Austin, Carson Looney, Bill Kreager, Jeff Speck, and Jim Wentling. Their comments were always sharp and to the point, reminding me that in housing, there are at least two sides to every question. Thanks also to Vincent Scully, who graciously agreed to review the manuscript and write the foreword.

There are many to thank at ULI. First, I would like to thank Michael Baker, David Mulvihill, and Adrienne Schmitz, each of whom authored a case study for this book. Their thoroughness and care are much appreciated. Adrienne Schmitz deserves a special thanks. In addition to authoring one of the case studies, Adrienne reviewed, revised, and coordinated production of the entire manuscript. For her many long hours, insightful comments, and dedication, I am grateful. Last, my appreciation goes to Gayle Berens, who helped frame the issues for this second edition, and who provided much-appreciated encouragement all the way through the process.

Steven Fader

contents

Foreword

This new edition of *Density by Design* shows a considerable advance in land planning and design since the first edition was published. This is due largely to the return to a denser, more integrated kind of community that has been developed over the past ten years. The new urbanism, a movement in architecture and town making hardly heard of a decade ago, now appears to be setting the standard for many of the best new housing developments and establishing the criteria by which they are being developed. These standards and criteria are well described by Steven Fader in his admirable introduction to this book, and there is no need to repeat them here, except to note that their major objective in every case is to encourage a sense of community, of neighborhood or town, rather than of "project" or "development."

Those qualities were all there in traditional American towns and in the American town planning of the first three decades of this century, as in the work of John Nolen and many others. The canonical modernism that came along in the 1930s, and later, did not value that tradition and effectively blotted out its memory for many years. The present movement is thus a revival of a way of shaping the environment that we once had and later lost.

Americans today seem to feel that a sense of community is exactly what needs to be revived in this country, and many apparently want exactly that for themselves and their families. It is therefore no great wonder that they are choosing to live in the kind of integrated architectural groupings that are suggestive of the towns in which they grew up, or about which they have always dreamed. Most of the case studies in this book seem to be trying to create such environments once more.

The new urbanist movement has been put together over the past 30 or so years by some of the best young architects in the United States. The creation of architecturally integrated communities, rather than that of a few knock-your-eye-out individual buildings, now has become a major preoccupation of a good part of the architectural profession. Andres Duany and Elizabeth Plater-Zyberk, trained at Princeton and Yale, first worked out—or rediscovered—the principles of town making with developer Robert Davis, when they created Seaside, Florida, which has become a prototype for town planners from all over the United States. Seaside seemed to be just what many people were waiting for. Now heavily overbuilt, it is swamped with clients who want to buy houses there, so that the original intention, which was to shape a simple Florida beach town on the gulf, has been considerably obscured. Houses selling for $150,000 or so ten years ago are today selling for around $500,000, and no end is in sight. Duany's objectives, like those of many of his colleagues, now look far beyond the rural or suburban settings of the first successes toward the center city itself and toward the kind of low- and moderate-income housing that makes sense for those who build it as well as those who live in it. Low-cost new urban communities already have replaced burned-out inner-city areas in places like the Nehemiah neighborhood in Cleveland, and elsewhere. This book offers good grounds for optimism in that regard. Several of the projects illustrated here show how the kind of density can be achieved that most, though by no means all, center cities require, and they do so largely in terms of the new urbanism.

History offers even greater hope. During World War I, the federal government built numerous emergency low-income housing groups, using the same principles of design that are reflected in this book: houses built in the vernacular of their region—cracker board and batten in Florida, colonial in New England—and arranged as villages related to the English garden-city movement but directly adapted to American images and styles of life. The single-family house, sensitively subdivided, as illustrated in several of the examples in this book, is a notable achievement, even when built at a sometimes surprisingly dense scale.

So it is that Seaside Park in Bridgeport, Connecticut, built in 1918 for the lowest paid workers in Bridgeport's great factories, is just as beautiful as Seaside, Florida, and just as loved and cared for by its inhabitants right up to today. As Duany says, "Once we did all this right in the United States." This book indicates that we are beginning to do so again.

Vincent Scully
Sterling Professor Emeritus of Art History
Yale University

introduction

Katherine Austin

1

Hayden Village, in Santa Rosa, California, provides affordable housing in a townlike development.

What is density? Is it good? Is it bad? The answers, of course, are relative to the context. Four dwelling units per acre may be dense in Montana, but 400 in Manhattan may not be. Or, to look at it another way, the density of Pruitt-Igoe, the notorious public housing complex in St. Louis (now demolished), was about the same as that of New York's eminently livable and attractive Greenwich Village neighborhood. "There is an anxiety about density," notes architect Alexander Seidel, whose work is featured in this book. But as Seidel concludes, it is not density itself that is the issue, but rather, "good or bad solutions to density." This book is about those solutions—about doing density well.

The problems we see around us are almost universally acknowledged: consumption of irreplaceable resources, disinvestment and deterioration of our cities, the loss of community, and the need to adapt to the demographics of a changing society. As a nation we are consuming millions of acres a year in new housing, converting farms, fields, and habitats into ever more distant subdivisions and communities. Back at the center, our cities continue to struggle, with the flight of capital easily outstripping new investment. And the new communities we are creating seem to lack the character and quality of the older towns and spaces we most admire.

These problems are not new. Suburbanization of the kind we call sprawl has been with us for a half century now, since the first large-scale subdivisions of the 1950s. And the deterioration of our cities, handmaiden to this mass suburbanization, has been around for as long. The critique of these problems has a pedigreed history, as well, from early works such as *The Costs of Sprawl* (Robert Burchell, 1974) and Jane Jacobs's *Death and Life of Great American Cities* (1961); through Peter Calthorpe's *The Next American Metropolis* (1993) and Peter Katz's *The New Urbanism* (1994). And the issue now has become very public. Suddenly, it seems, the "livability" question is mainstream. News weeklies such as *Time* and *Newsweek* have featured it, and the issue has become a topic of political discourse.

As many commentators have noted, the issues of sprawl and urban deterioration are not unrelated. These twin poles of our urban condition rise and fall on macroeconomics and politics: the cost of land, the hidden subsidies for highway development, exclusionary zoning, and the like. Builders and designers work within a market and a political context that tend to favor sprawl over compact development, and urban disintegration over reinvestment. It is clear that a complete and satisfactory answer to these issues lies beyond the capacity of individual builders or designers working on single projects within this market-driven context. Yet there are many ways developers and architects are attempting to deal with these issues and to minimize the adverse impacts of growth.

Increased density is one way. Spurred by the necessity of holding the line on land costs, but increasingly attuned to the issues of community and livability, developers and architects are experimenting with building more compact communities: smaller lot sizes, smaller streets, more efficient parking, and integrally designed public open spaces and community facilities. They are also looking at ways to increase the intensity of land use: for example, accessory dwelling units over garages, and residential uses—live/work units and lofts—intermixed with retail uses.

The mixing of residential and retail uses is tied into the goal of reducing auto dependency:

2, 3

The Crossings, in Mountain View, California, is a transit-oriented, walkable community that combines single-family residences, townhomes, and condominiums.

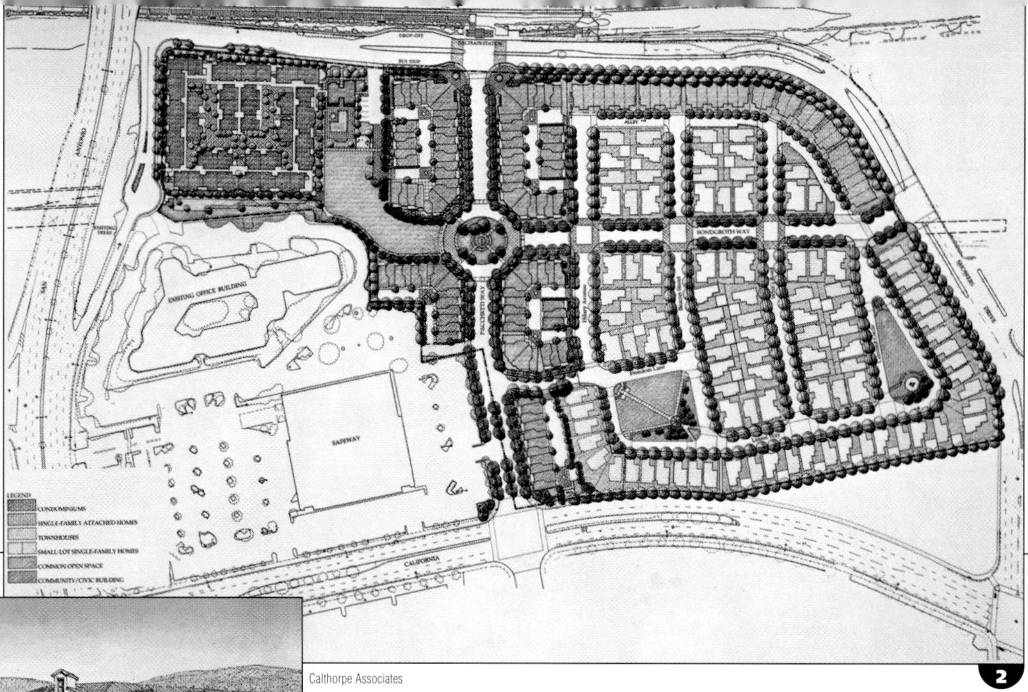

Calthorpe Associates

Calthorpe Associates

by designing walkable communities—the five-minute neighborhood—designers are attempting, in an incipient way, to break the habit of automobile use. On a larger scale, increasing attention is being paid to developing housing in concert with transit policy. The concept of transit-oriented development (TOD) promoted by Peter Calthorpe and others is gaining currency, and many examples now exist, including Orenco Station and others discussed in this book.

Perhaps the greatest recent change to the ethos of housing production lies in what has to be called a reawakening to the communal realm. Inspired by the theories and increasing practice of the new urbanism, the social and spiritual significance of public space—everything from streets and sidewalks to public buildings and neighborhood centers—is being reexamined. And this reexamination ranges from the most global—for example, the symbolism inherent in the siting of a public building—to the most technologically narrow—the minimum street width in which a fire truck can reasonably navigate.

There is a new search for meaning in our physical environment. What is sacred ground? What is social ground? What does the formality of an axial boulevard tell us? What emotional reassurance is there in a vista terminated by a school or a monument? Community designers are focusing anew on the symbolic import of streets—the use of street design to create a hierarchy of meaning, not just a hierarchy of traffic flow; using streets and open space to define neighborhoods and to link them. And the placement of public buildings—the conscious design of where civic elements should be—is an art, once common, that is now being rediscovered.

Concurrent with this is a new quest for community, a searching for the physical factors that facilitate social interaction and foster a sense of communal satisfaction. Both applauded and derided, the front porch has become the symbol of this new direction. Increasingly, houses are being sited closer to the street, garages banished to the rear or recessed, and front porches mandated, in an attempt to revive or ignite the sense of sociability and connectedness that post–World War II neighborhoods seem to have lost.

On a more prosaic level, post–World War II concepts of street design are being challenged—

Marshall Erdman & Associates

Photo: © Steve Hinds

RTKL/Craig Balckmon

specifically, the cul-de-sac, symbol of an earlier generation of suburban housing. Newer theories and empirical studies of street safety argue that a more uniform network of streets is both safer and more empowering for those without a car. Street width also has become a battleground. In the name of safer streets and more intimate communities, as well as land conservation and reduced development costs, developers and designers have been challenging prevailing public works and fire department standards for street widths, which have expanded over the years along with lot sizes and houses.

The return to community is being fought on another level as well. Challenging the single-use planning and zoning mentality that has been the hallmark of contemporary development, a variety of projects, both urban and suburban, are testing the waters with mixed land use, mixed housing types, and mixed lot sizes in close proximity. The idea of a mixed-use neighborhood/town center, with shops and services below and housing above, is an old—even ancient—concept that is being revived by a new generation of planners and designers. The neighborhood/town center concept holds the potential appeal both of restoring a sense of community and supporting an environmentalist agenda.

Established suburbs and edge cities are becoming denser and mixing even more uses through infill and redevelopment of strategic properties. This increased density springs, in many cases, not only from the imperatives of real estate economics, but also from a political desire to establish a focus or identity for the jurisdiction—the sense of place that never materialized in an earlier rush to build. Some of these new projects, such as Addison Circle near Dallas, are finding a ready reception from a newly emerging market segment: renters by choice. Developers like Post Properties of Atlanta are finding that both suburban towns and urban areas have a barely tapped market of young to middle-aged prospects, as well as

4

Middleton Hills, in Middleton, Wisconsin, embodies the principles of the new urbanism with its small setbacks, front porches, and rear garages.

5, 6

Increasingly, new development opens to the street, often mixing first-level retail with housing. Both Riverside in Atlanta, Georgia (photo 5), and Addison Circle in Addison, Texas (photo 6), successfully employ first-floor retail with apartments above.

Backen Arrigoni & Ross/Douglas Dun

empty nesters and retirees, who have relatively high incomes but still choose to rent and who find an urban (and urbane) environment more appealing than a garden apartment complex.

This issue of urban livability is addressed by several of the projects profiled in this book. In the wide wake of Oscar Newman's eye-opening book, *Defensible Space*, both suburban and urban projects are more consciously being designed to "engage the street." Rather than turning inward—the fortress mentality prevalent in recent years—developers are increasingly designing projects that open up to the street, with individual townhouse entries and old-fashioned front stoops. And many new projects are providing such street-level amenities as neighborhood retail, services, and outdoor dining.

Developers also are focusing on niche markets. There is a noticeable back-to-the city movement in many parts of the country, encouraged by lowered crime rates and improved economies. On one end of the market, there are younger households that are providing support for more "edgy" loftlike projects, both adaptive use projects and new mid- and high-rise buildings. On the other end of the spectrum, developers are finding success with large urban townhouses and condominiums built to the size of single-family detached houses and marketed to suburban empty nesters who are attracted by the prospect of city living after years of suburban life.

While new construction appears to be picking up steam in urban areas, preservation remains an alternative option for many cities. Although federal tax incentives are not as large as they once were, the wealth of empty or underused historic structures in cities remains a nearly priceless asset waiting to be put back into useful service. Adaptive use is not, of course, a new idea, but the range of buildings now being converted offers new possibilities for housing and community revitalization.

Each in its own way, the 14 case studies in this book address these themes; they are the stories of projects that attempt to deal with the issues of sprawl, urban reinvestment, and the quality of life. They range from freestanding new suburban communities to edge city infill to urban reconstruction and preservation. All have advanced beyond the paper stage, and most are substantially or completely built out. They represent not just theoretical approaches to the issues, but approaches that have survived the test of both the approvals process and the marketplace.

The case studies include single-family detached prototypes, townhouses, and multifamily housing, as well as varying combinations and hybrids. The cases include for-sale and rental projects, both market-rate and subsidized. A primary emphasis is the public context of

8

Looney Ricks Kiss Architects, Inc.

housing: site planning, lot layout standards, parking, street configurations, and architecture. At the unit level, the cases emphasize trends in dwelling unit design, particularly in the way that housing is being adapted to changing demographics, employment, and social preferences.

The selected projects are more densely developed than the norm—clearly a key to solving many of the problems described above. But they are not necessarily the most dense of their types; rather, they were chosen because they reflect a more holistic approach to the problems of housing and community development, and because they represent a level of design sophistication that goes beyond what is typical for production or builder housing.

The case study approach and format adopted for this book also are intended to highlight emerging quantitative standards for the basic building blocks of housing and community development: for example, lot sizes, setback standards, street and alley dimensions, and parking ratios. The case studies, in that sense, represent a snapshot of housing at the millennium, revealing where we are now and where we may be going. These emerging standards and directions, summarized in the following pages, will provide a useful benchmark for planners, builders, and designers as we enter the 21st century.

Eakin/Youngentob

9

7

Paseo Plaza, urban infill in San Jose, California.

8

Harbor Town, a new urbanist community in Memphis, Tennessee.

9

Courthouse Square, residential infill in Arlington, Virginia.

single-family detached housing

The Single-Family Lot

The basic building block of single-family housing, and the chief determinant of density, is the single-family-detached lot. Because of cost—and in some cases, for policy reasons—the single-family lot is getting smaller. There are still plenty of large-lot subdivisions, of course, but the trend toward smaller lot sizes is continuing. "Ten years ago," notes Bill Kreager, principal of Mithun Partners, Inc., a Seattle-based architecture firm, "a 7,200-square-foot lot was embarrassingly small." Today, lots as small as 2,500 square feet are being widely marketed, and in some "affordable" housing projects, lot sizes are even smaller.

Older, pre–World War II single-family-detached suburbs were often platted in 50-foot increments: typically a 50-foot by 100-foot (5,000 square feet) lot, usually accommodating a single-car garage at the rear. In the postwar years, suburban lot sizes grew, along with the ubiquitous two-car garage, to a width of 70 feet or more in many cases. A quarter-acre, or 10,000-square-foot, lot became the norm in many suburban communities.

More recently, and particularly in the 1990s, lot sizes have been retreating, with 25- to 40-foot widths becoming increasingly common. At Middleton Hills, for example, a traditional neighborhood development (TND) in Middleton, Wisconsin, the smallest single-family lots are 32 feet wide by 80 feet deep (2,560 square feet). And at Harbor Town, in Memphis, Tennessee, some lots are as small as 25 feet by 100 feet (2,500 square feet). The theoretical "yield" on such lots, exclusive of streets and other public spaces, is 17.4 units per acre.[1]

A related trend is the mixing of lot sizes within a development—not just at the project level, but at the microlevel of the street or block. At Harbor Town, for example, 2,500-square-foot lots with $130,000 houses in some cases sit adjacent to 5,500-square-foot lots with $800,000 houses. The key to the successful mixing of house sizes and income strata at Harbor Town and similar communities, according to Carson Looney of Looney Ricks Kiss (LRK) Architects, is "the establishment of design guidelines that ensure the compatible scale, proportion, detailing, and quality for both small houses and large." While not everyone agrees that mixing lot sizes and product types is desirable from a market perspective, the concept has the potential for increasing overall densities within single-family subdivisions.

Lot Layout

Houses are moving forward on their lots, influenced both by TND principles and by shrinking lot sizes. Front setbacks as small as 10 or 20 feet are not uncommon in small-lot subdivisions and new communities. The reintroduction of the front porch, which is usually permitted to encroach forward of the setback line, is part of this concept, compensating, to some extent, for smaller units and smaller lots. From the new urbanist perspective, bringing the house closer to the street encourages sociability and helps to create community, though there are many in the housing industry that would dispute this notion.

With the front yard foreshortened and the rear yard increasingly used for parking and access, the side yard is assuming the role once exclusively held by the backyard. In the side yard

[1]43,560 square feet ÷ 2,500 square feet = 17.4 units per acre (not including streets).

10, 11

Prototype single-family houses by Calthorpe Associates show how lot sizes can be mixed in a single block, without compromising design integrity. Each house includes a front porch, rear outdoor space, and a single or double garage, pushed to the rear of the lot.

12

Lots at Orenco Station illustrate the passive use easement concept, a variation on zero-lot-lines.

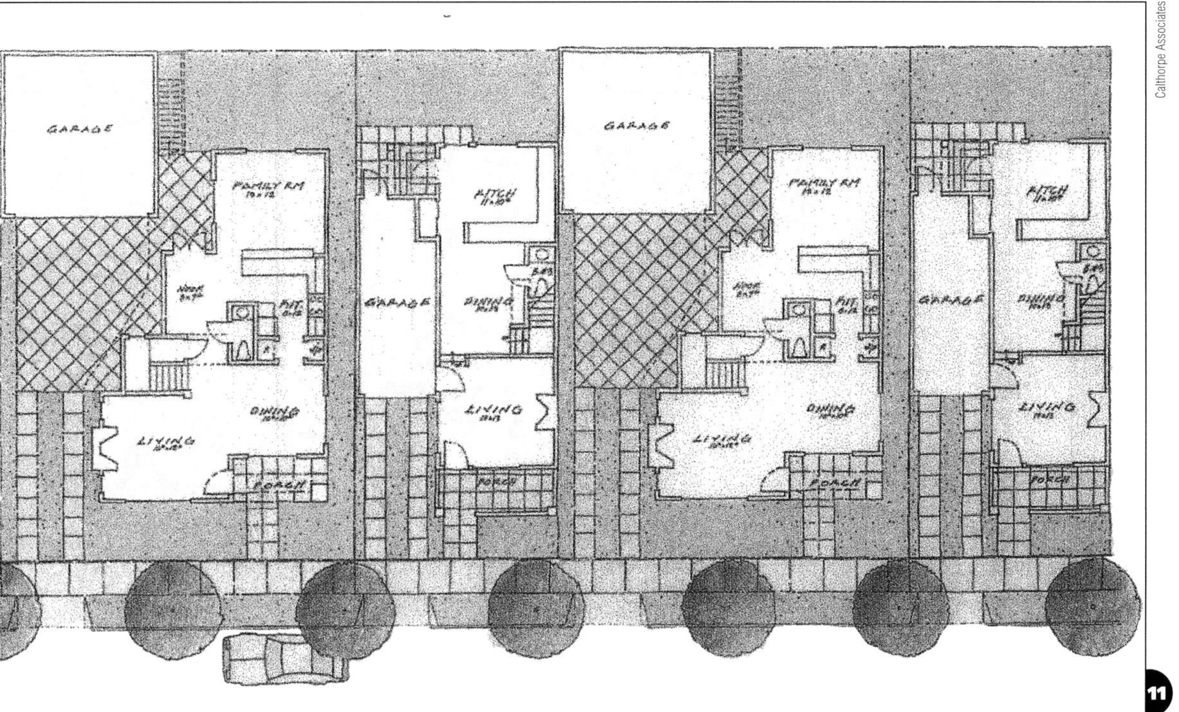

Calthorpe Associates

model, the dwelling unit is pushed to one side of the lot and elongated. Often—as in the side yard houses at Harbor Town, which are patterned after colonial-era "Charleston single houses"—the unit designs are one room wide, with doors and windows from several rooms opening onto side porches and then to patios or landscaped courtyards. As these side yard spaces are narrow—sometimes just 10 to 20 feet wide—large expanses of lawn are less feasible. At their best, the spaces tend to be treated more carefully, as in a Japanese garden, balancing hardscape and landscape. When windows are allowed on the adjacent house's side elevation, privacy is maintained by setting the windows high on the wall relative to floor levels, allowing for light penetration but limiting the view into the neighboring yard.

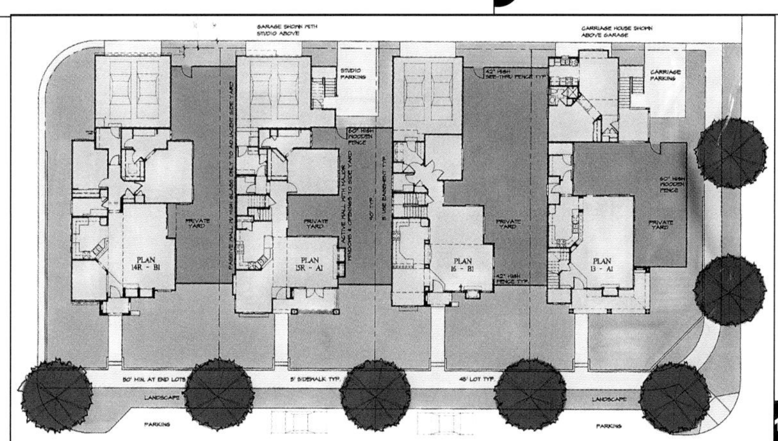

Iverson Associates, Inc.

Looney Ricks Kiss Architects, Inc.

Many of the new side yard houses follow the "passive use" easement concept, a newer variation on the zero-lot-line concept that has been around for many years. In the zero-lot-line model, each house is located on the side yard property line to allow the maximum use of the remaining side yard. A limitation of this model is that fire and building codes prohibit windows on the lot line wall, and require that the wall be one-hour fire-rated. In the passive use easement model, the houses are shifted three to five feet in from the property line, allowing for windows on all elevations. The space lost to the usable side of the lot as the house is shifted is recaptured by the grant of an easement to use the adjacent three- to five-foot setback of the neighboring house.

Parking: Alley Access

After many years of front-loaded two-car garages dominating the residential streetscape, the treatment of parking has become the subject of much experimentation. One of the more controversial trends has been the return to alley-loaded parking. To its adherents, alley parking offers multiple benefits: it removes the architectural dominance of the garage on the streetscape, and it eliminates individual curb cuts at each house, thereby returning more street frontage to on-street parking. When on-street parking is made more efficient, it is sometimes possible to eliminate parking on one side of the street and thereby narrow the width of the street. Countering this, some builders argue that alley-loaded parking is like building streets on both sides of the house, driving up costs to the consumer. Others have questioned the long-term maintenance of these "back door" spaces and even the desirability of substituting rear driveway access for the more public front driveway.

Development standards for residential alleys (also called drive lanes or parking lanes for marketing purposes) are varied. The typical alley tends to be about 24 feet wide from

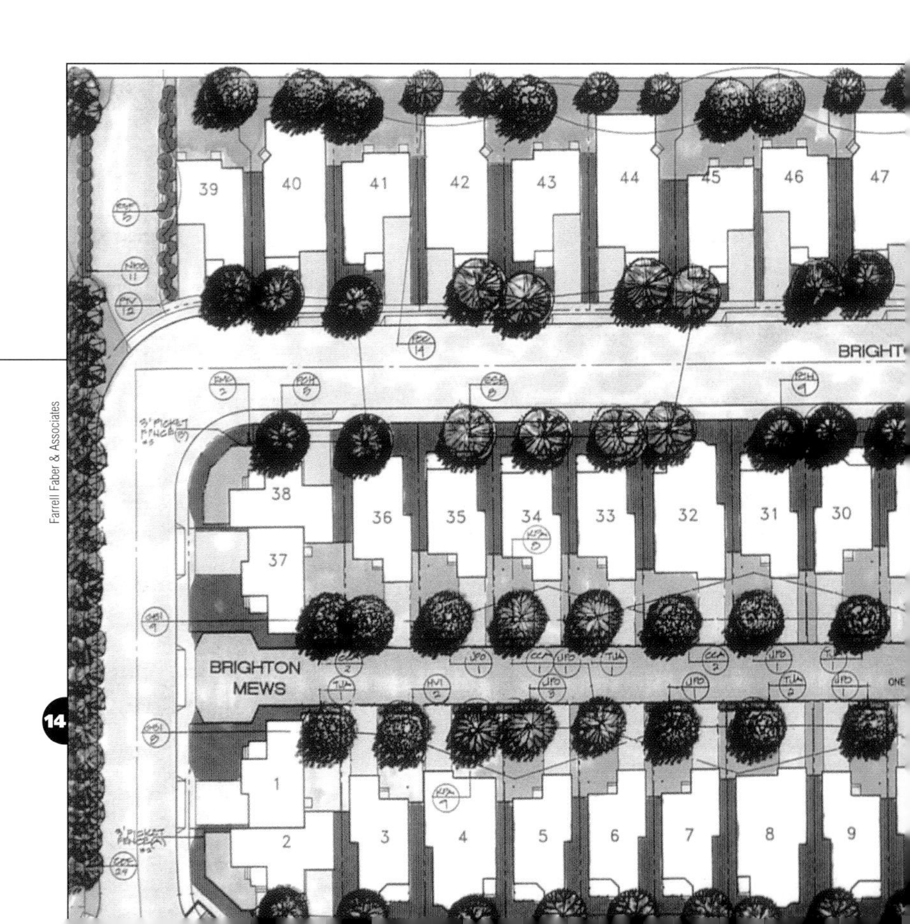

Farrell Faber & Associates

13

Rear garages with alley access at Harbor Town.

14

An alley (shown on right) provides rear garage access to about half of the units in Hayden Village, Santa Rosa, California.

15

Metro Senior Housing & CityPark in Foster City, California, was the result of a creative approach to mixed housing. Market-rate townhouses and assisted seniors' housing share mews access.

16

When three-car garages are demanded by the market, there are design solutions that can be accommodated on narrow lots to improve the view from the street. Some of these involve splitting the garage into two garages sited on a landscaped courtyard, or including a tandem garage space.

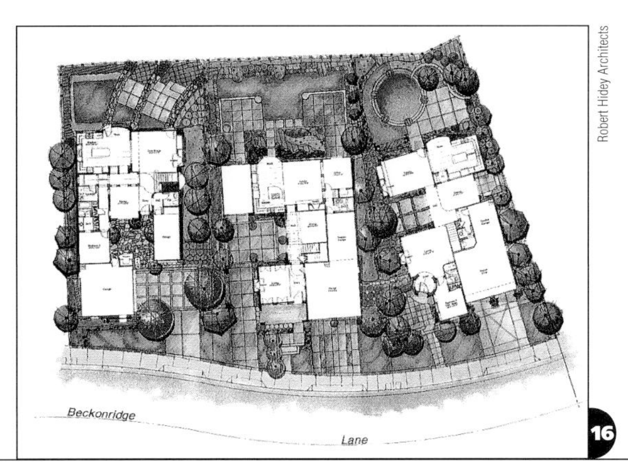

Robert Hidey Architects

Seidel/Holzman

garage face to garage face, of which 10 to 20 feet are usually paved, allowing for a landscape buffer on either side. In some cases, as at Orenco Station in Hillsboro, Oregon, alleys provide the principal access for accessory units over garages. These units have windows and porches overlooking the alleys, providing "eyes on the street."

Other Parking Models

A second approach to the issue of parking is shared driveway access to recessed parking courts. Amberleigh, located in Mill Creek, Washington, takes this approach. Designed for empty nesters, the project's fourplex units share a single curb cut and driveway. The driveway leads back to a parking court that gives access to each unit's two-car garage. As with alley parking, the garages are taken out of the streetscape and hidden from view.

A third model is the set-back garage. In a return to a pre–World War II mode, some developers and municipalities are opting for front-accessed garages set toward the rear of the lot. In the Santa Rosa, California, small-lot ordinance, for example, one covered parking space is required on each lot, set back at least 20 feet, which then allows a second car to park in front of it. In other cases, developers have tried two-car tandem garages although this configuration has not been widely replicated.

Counter to the small-lot trend is the increasing demand for three-car garages, a particularly vexing problem from a design point of view. Developers are responding to this challenge in several ways including: rotating the garage 90 degrees to the street to minimize the bulk and appearance of the garage doors; dressing the turned face in the design vocabulary of the house, including windows; and splitting the garage into two separate masses for architectural effect. An example of the last technique is Port Ivy, a subdivision in southern California. In this Mediterranean-influenced project, the split garages are arranged to create courtyard-type open spaces as part of the home's entrance or side yard.

The Home Office

Inside the home, one of the most significant trends in housing design is the increasing accommodation of those who work at home. Some 23 million of us were working at home, at least part-time, as of 1997[2]; that number is expected to rise sharply in coming years.

At its most minimal, the home office is a computer niche (often an open area at the top of a stairway) or an alcove between rooms—small spaces that tend to make the house feel larger and also serve as work space. At the other end of the scale is the completely enclosed office, sometimes located over a detached garage, designed and wired for telecommuting or home-based businesses.

[2] "Work at Home in 1997," Bureau of Labor Statistics news release, 1998.

Roy H. Kruse & Associates/Robert J. Heidrich

17

Some sections of the Pointe at Lincoln Park in Chicago share common garages under the residences. From the garages, residents have direct private entrances to the units.

18

At Orenco Station, optional space over the garage can be finished as a studio or accessory unit. The separate space has its own entrance and overlooks the rear alley.

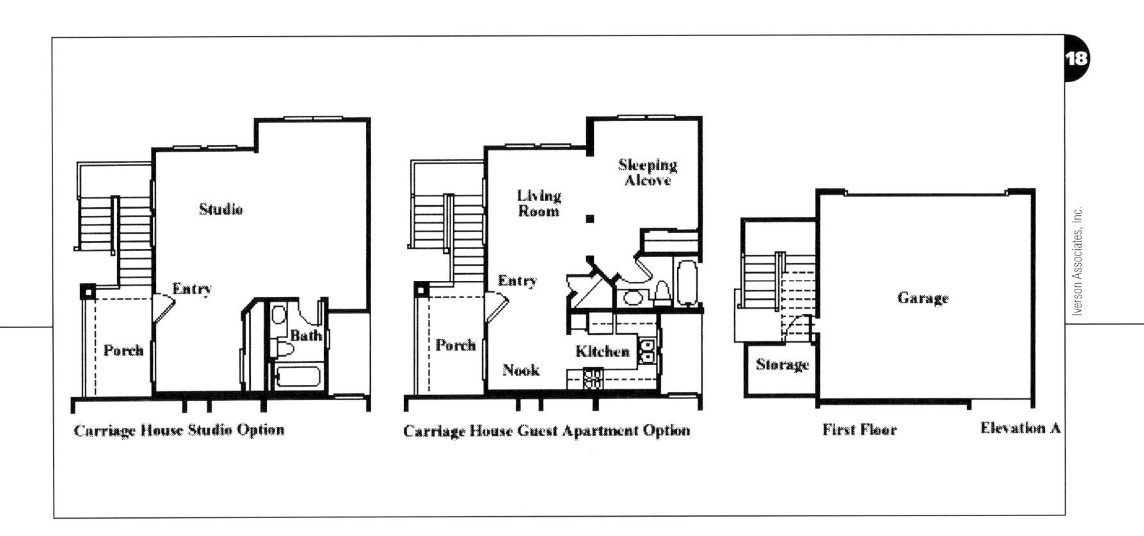

Exemplifying the latter is "Blueprint 2000," a prototypical home of the year for the new century, designed by LRK Architects for *Better Homes and Gardens*. The Blueprint 2000 house provides for an office above a detached garage, separated from the main residence but connected to it by a covered arcade.

In between these poles are "flex" spaces, or "swing rooms," as they are sometimes called. The living room, which over time has become a smaller, formal parlor, is now being eliminated altogether by some builders, and replaced by the flex room, whose basic purpose is to provide a place to work, be it for schoolwork, paying the bills, or telecommuting. Because it is more of a "work" room than a "show" room, the flex space sometimes is moved back from the front hall, often positioned adjacent to the kitchen or between the kitchen and garage.

Accessory Units

The accessory dwelling unit—a small, secondary, self-contained dwelling unit, often called a "granny flat" or "carriage home"—is both old news and new. Typically 400 to 500 square feet in size and located above the garage, accessory units have been advocated for many years, but for the most part have not been permitted by local zoning codes, for reasons ranging from fire prevention to exclusionary zoning intent. As planners and designers have long noted, accessory units can help advance the following objectives: increase density; provide affordable housing for new or small households; allow for intergenerational independence (literally housing "granny," or perhaps a grown son or daughter); provide usable space for the owner to build out as household income grows; and provide separately accessed space for home office or a similar use. Accessory units also may increase affordability for the purchaser of the primary dwelling through the rental income generated by the accessory unit, although lenders have sometimes been reluctant to recognize this income.

The news is that accessory units are beginning to become available. What it has taken is a rewriting of zoning law, jurisdiction by jurisdiction. Often this is being achieved in conjunction with the adoption of a new, more flexible design code, or in some cases within the more limited approvals for a specific planned development proposal. Where accessory units have been tried, the market reaction has been varied. At Orenco Station, for example, about 30 percent of those who bought a unit that offered the choice have exercised the option to build a "carriage home." Some have rented out the unit, in true granny flat fashion, and others have kept the space for their own use—everything from a hobby room to a guest bedroom. Although still in the early stages of trial, both at Orenco Station and elsewhere, the accessory unit concept can be expected to gain currency as this type of housing acquires more of a track record.

19

At Courthouse Hill, mid-rise condominium buildings are positioned to soften the edges among neighboring high-rise buildings, the more pedestrian-scaled new development, and the existing low-rise residential neighborhood.

20

At Celebration, Florida, the Gables rental housing engages the street. Garages are tucked behind.

Lessard Architectural Group

19

Mixed Housing

The grip of single-use zoning is loosening in other ways, as well. Mixed housing subdivisions and new communities—mixed by type of housing, tenure, price, and household income—are increasing. With the goal of creating diverse and self-contained communities, developers—with municipal concurrence and sometimes insistence—are creating opportunities for mixed housing. Sometimes this is a matter of varying lot sizes, in order to get variation within a single housing type. An example is the lot size and price point mixing of single-family housing at Harbor Town. Other increasingly common variations include mixing of single-family housing with townhouses, combinations of for-sale and rental housing, and mixing of market-rate and subsidized housing. The aspect that is new is not that of including multiple housing types within a single project, which planned communities have been doing for some time, but rather that of integrating varying market segments within small neighborhood units (a single block or street, for example) as is common in pre–World War II towns and cities.

A case that illustrates the concept is Metro Senior Housing & CityPark in suburban Foster City, California. The program for this project called for market-rate for-sale townhouses and subsidized seniors' rental housing in a mid-rise configuration. The available site for the project actually was two noncontiguous parcels, and the usual response would have been to devote each parcel to a single use for a single market segment: townhouses on one, seniors on the other. But in a successful test of the increasing sophistication of the market, the designers

RTKL/Paris Rutherford

20

put both uses on both parcels, wrapping the townhouses around the seniors' building and sharing access to both. Alexander Seidel, the project's designer, notes that the townhouse portion of the project experienced "no discernible loss of value in the marketplace from being close to the assisted housing."

A second example, in a more urban context, is Crawford Square, a redevelopment project in Pittsburgh, Pennsylvania. Here, single-family, townhouse, and apartment buildings were mixed within a few square blocks. Some of the units are for-sale, some rental, some market-rate, and some subsidized housing, but the market segments are not segregated one from the other. In this case, the key to success was that no visual distinctions were made in the housing designs to signal the type of housing tenure: a rental townhouse looks like a for-sale townhouse. Further, within the pool of rental units, subsidized units are rotated periodically, preventing any stigma from being attached to specific units.

attached housing prototypes

Townhouses

As the principal mid-density alternative to single-family detached housing, townhouses are being used in a wide variety of contexts. In suburban locations, attached housing is being integrated increasingly with single-family housing to increase overall project densities. Townhouses are also being used increasingly in urban projects (often mixed with still higher density housing types) to maintain a pedestrian-oriented presence on the street. At Courthouse Hill, in Arlington, Virginia, for example, townhouses are combined with mid-rise condominiums to provide a pedestrian-scaled project while still yielding an overall density of 44 units per acre.

As is true for single-family detached housing, much of the current design exploration has to do with parking. As land becomes more scarce and expensive, developers increasingly tuck parking underneath the units and build higher. At Metro Senior Housing & CityPark, for example, living quarters are on the second and third levels, with a two-car garage below, accessed via a brick-paved alley driveway. The idea of a "mews" is a variant on this theme. Originally narrow cartways flanked by stables, in their current incarnation, mews are being designed as semiprivate drive lanes or walkways cut into the grid of the city block, providing access to garages or pedestrian entrances to townhouses, which flank the mews on either side.

A third variation is the use of communal garages—either at grade or below—tucked under a row or double row of townhouses. In order to increase density at the Pointe at Lincoln Park, in Chicago, some of the townhouses are built back to back, with some units

Fisher-Friedman Architects

21

facing the street and others facing an interior courtyard. Parking is in a common garage structure under the townhouses, with entries at either end of the townhouse row.

The other way to increase density, of course, is to build vertically. While some of the units at the Pointe are built back to back, others are stacked: two-story townhouses over two-story townhouses. Beyond four stories, elevators are required, and the unit type usually becomes a flat (one-level apartment unit). Paseo Plaza in downtown San Jose, California, is an example of a townhouse/flat hybrid. The first two floors of Paseo are two-story townhouse-type units, above which are four levels of flats.

Like many new projects, Paseo Plaza uses the idea of a full-block closure to define public space and private space. Facing the street, the townhouses have individual entries, gardens, and stoops. The intent is to provide an inviting pedestrian streetscape but also one that will be monitored by residents. The interior of the block, in contrast, is a wholly private open space, accessible only to residents and guests.

Loft Housing

The loft, as a dwelling unit type, is moving from the province of artist housing into the mainstream of commercially viable developer housing. Once restricted to adaptive use

21

Old brick is the background for the sleek steel and glass entrance at Oriental Warehouse, an adaptive use development in San Francisco.

22

In New York's financial district, the Exchange recycled a century-old office building as luxury rental apartments.

projects in a few select cities, like San Francisco and New York, loftlike units are finding a broader market in both new construction and old, in locations around the country. Much of this response is driven by the architecture: loft projects, with their two-story spaces and often raw finishes and industrial materials, have an appeal not found in the typical condominium, not to mention the single-family house.

For adaptive use projects, some of the appeal lies in the juxtaposition of new and old materials: white drywall against brick, for example, or stainless steel counters against aged wooden beams and heavy timber posts. Part of the attraction is the configuration of space. The openness—the sheer amount of space—often substantially exceeds that of new construction.

Developers are finding success in new loft construction as well as in adaptive use. Site 17, a new eight-story building in Seattle, for example, included a double floor of loft units, with bare concrete floors, raw steel door frames, and exposed mechanical ducting, all within 720- to 990-square-foot units. Their small size and minimal finish made the units more affordable, and the raw look ("lofts and apartments with attitude," says the project's brochure) made the units more appealing to the young market in Seattle's arts district. Commenting on urban markets in general, Tim Abell of Harbor Properties, Site 17's developer, notes,"The demand [from the young urban market] just isn't being met by the stucco boxes."

Adaptive Use

Like loft housing, the adaptive use of historic structures is expanding. A wide array of building types—not just industrial structures—is now being pressed into service for housing, and the market for adaptive use continues to grow. The three examples of adaptive use in this book span the range of recent projects. The Oriental Warehouse is an upscale project of 66 live/work, for-sale housing units. The project was constructed almost from scratch within the shell of an old brick warehouse. The Cotton Mill in New Orleans, Louisiana, in contrast, is primarily a rental project that relied on the gritty qualities of the old mill—the mottled layers of paint and industrial artifacts—to market smaller apartments and lofts to a younger age group. The third adaptive use case study is a high-rise office building, the 22-story Exchange in lower Manhattan, converted to luxury rental apartments. Although the difficulties of adaptive use are in some ways increasing—hazardous materials abatement requirements are becoming more stringent, agency oversight is becoming more demanding, and tax policy is not as favorable as it once was—these projects demonstrate the market feasibility, and from a policy point of view, the desirability, of adaptive use as a housing strategy.

23

Plan for Seaside, Florida.

24, 25

In Celebration, Florida, Market Street, in the town center, has street-level shops and restaurants with apartments on upper levels. On-street parking lines both sides of the street, which culminates at a pedestrian plaza along a manmade lake.

community design

©The Walt Disney Company

Site Design

A noticeable formality has come back into site design after years of curving streets and subdivision "informality." The trend harkens back to a more beaux-arts view of urban design, using streets to organize and give meaning to the urban fabric. The use of diagonal boulevards and axiality has become more common, based on the models of Seaside, Florida, and other early new urbanist communities. Coupled with the notion of axiality is the idea of the termination of vistas—the formal completion of the processional set up by the diagonal or axial boulevard or street.

These concepts are illustrated by several of the case studies in this book, from the formal pergola that completes the view along Orenco

Duany Plater-Zyberk & Company

Station's Main Street to the prominent axial sites reserved for public buildings in the Middleton Hills master plan. In a similar manner, the device of a diagonal boulevard is used at Addison Circle, near Dallas, Texas, to link the major commercial and residential subareas of that project. The diagonal also is used to great effect at Harbor Town, as a means to open up views of the Mississippi River and the Memphis skyline.

Off the boulevard, the popular cul-de-sac prototype is being challenged by some designers and theorists. The argument against the cul-de-sac is that it forces high volumes of traffic onto collector and arterial streets, which then become traffic choked and unsafe barriers for children and others without auto mobility. The alternative, illustrated by Middleton Hills, Harbor Town, and other projects, is a "network solution": making all streets through-streets, to distribute traffic and reduce the need for high-speed, high-capacity collectors. Although the local network streets carry more traffic than cul-de-sac streets, the argument is that, overall, the network opens up a wider territory to safe access and use by children, the elderly, and others without cars. Most builders still find that homebuyers perceive the cul-de-sac as the safer and more desirable alternative, although experimentation with network street design is beginning to generate market support for this concept.

Street Width

The movement toward reducing local street widths is gaining ground. In the 1920s, typical local streets had a 28- to 30-foot curb-to-curb dimension, allowing two-way traffic and parking on both sides. By the 1950s, the typical suburban street had grown to a width of 36 feet, and this standard has been fiercely defended by public works departments and fire departments across the country. The wider streets, it has been argued, are necessary to handle traffic flow, to accommodate fire trucks, and even to facilitate civil defense evacuation. But tests conducted in older neighborhoods have confirmed the workability of the older model, and municipalities slowly are backing away from the expanded width standards.

The rationale for narrower streets is persuasive: they are less costly to build, and therefore contribute to housing affordability; narrower streets consume less land and preserve vegetation; they produce less stormwater runoff; they contribute to a more compact neighborhood, which can encourage pedestrian trips over auto use; and recent testing indicates that a narrower right-of-way slows traffic, and is therefore safer.[3]

The city of Portland, Oregon, has been a leader in the movement toward narrowing streets. The city's "Skinny Streets" program allows for 26-foot, two-way streets with parking on both sides, and 20-foot-wide streets with parking on one side. Similarly, developers of several of the case study projects described in this book have negotiated street widths of 28 feet or less.

Sidewalks and Planting Strips

As streets are getting narrower, sidewalks are growing. While the four-foot-wide sidewalk remains standard in suburban development, some developers and some communities are moving to a four-and-a-half- or five-foot minimum as a more pedestrian-friendly standard. The wider standard is based on the width considered appropriate for two persons walking abreast.

More attention is also being paid to the planting strip usually located between the curb and the sidewalk. To foster a more mature look, developers in some cases are providing larger, more mature trees at the outset, or planting the trees at closer intervals. In some cases, as at Addison Circle, the municipality is contributing to the cost of the higher-than-usual level of street landscaping. In other cases, in order to promote housing affordability, municipalities are allowing the planting strip to be located on the opposite side of the sidewalk, contiguous with the private lot, giving the appearance, if not the reality, of a larger property.

[3] For example, see *Residential Street Typology and Injury Accident Frequency*, a study by Swift and Associates and the city of Longmont, Colorado, 1997.

The Neighborhood/Town Center

The prospect of an intimate neighborhood main street, and the ability to walk to it, underlies much new planning; the partial experience of it—even the anticipation of it—has had noticeable consumer appeal. The planning objectives for neighborhood/town centers are typically multiple: to create a pedestrian-oriented environment and thereby reduce auto use and dependency; to create community identity and vibrancy; and to provide alternative housing choices—for example, live/work housing and accessible housing for seniors. And, recognizing the emergence of home offices and their potential social downside, new urbanist Andres Duany adds another rationale for neighborhood centers: "Now, more than ever," he comments, "town centers are needed to mitigate the social isolation of working at home."

John Schleimer, Market Perspectives 26

Although the idea of a neighborhood or town center has wide appeal, implementation is usually a challenge. It is often quite difficult to lease neighborhood retail space before the neighborhood or community grows large enough to support it. And from a developer's point of view, not all who want to lease space would make appropriate tenants, given the image and mix of tenants desired. In order to create the desired mix, and to overcome the reluctance of some retailers to participate in this concept, developers in some cases have taken to subsidizing initial retail tenant rents.

Most developers wait until a critical population mass is in place before starting the neighborhood center. At Orenco Station, for example, some 200 dwelling units were built before the first shop opened. Others have taken a different approach. The developer of Middleton Hills strategically planted the neighborhood center flag by constructing a 10,000-square-foot retail/office building before there were more than a handful of homes constructed. While the building is only partially occupied, it contains a general store and the neighborhood's central mail pickup. It is intended as a symbol of the community that one day will be built.

Part of the leasing issue—both positive and negative—has to do with the physical design of the neighborhood/town center. Although the recently opened first phase of Orenco Station's town center has been quite successful and well received, Mike Mehaffy, project manager for PacTrust, the developer, notes that the center "violates longstanding principles of suburban development." By this he means that the parking is located in the rear instead of being prominently on view from the street.

In lieu of a strip mall surrounded by a parking lot, Orenco Station, like many new communities, has sought to create a more pedestrian-oriented environment, closer in spirit to the main streets of older towns. Sidewalks in the Orenco Station town center are 16 feet wide (larger in some places), and ground floor retail spaces have roll-up glass doors that open up to outdoor dining. Three restaurants have opened, along with a coffee shop and other small shops and businesses. Success is not without cost, however. Given the extensive research and development, the code compliance issues that surround mixed-use development, and the more intensive design and consulting requirements, developing a successful mixed-use neighborhood or town center remains a more complicated (and therefore expensive) process than the strip mall alternative.

RTKL/Paris Rutherford 27

Ed Hershberger

26
Pergola in a park at Orenco Station, Portland, Oregon.
27
Addison Circle draws pedestrian activity to its main streets.
28
Orenco Station's town center includes housing on upper floors.

Live/Work Housing

An integral element of many new neighborhood/town centers is live/work housing. The term "live/work," now current, is shorthand for what used to be called "living above the shop." In its current incarnation, however, the shop is defined more widely, not only as retail businesses but also as professional offices, service businesses, and even new technology-based businesses. Even though it harkens back to a familiar past, this housing type has had little recent experience, particularly in suburbia.

The first phase of construction on Orenco Station's town center housing—12 live/work units and 16 loft-type townhouses over ground floor retail—has been completed. With the first units sold, Dick Loffelmacher of PacTrust notes,"There is a market for this type of development, even in suburban Hillsboro (Oregon)," although the contours of this market—its breadth and depth—are only beginning to be explored.

Future Trends

What will the next ten years bring? The housing industry is notably decentralized and slow to change, but even so, there is a clear movement toward restoring the balance between the private and public realms. There is a new emphasis on the quality of life that goes beyond the confines of the individual house and backyard. For new suburbs, this means more strongly integrating land planning and architecture and giving more careful attention to the transportation and community aspects of design. For existing suburbs and edge cities, it means focusing infill development and redevelopment efforts on creating identity and a sense of place. And for urban areas, it means building neighborhoods, not just projects.

The issues of density and community, much discussed in this book, are interrelated. When well executed, "density brings community and security," notes Bill Kreager, a Seattle architect. And "the emphasis on community," he continues, "is a remarkable tool for making people comfortable with higher densities." The 14 case studies that follow demonstrate, in real terms, both the complexities and the opportunities that these issues represent.

case studies

case study

Middleton Hills

Middleton, Wisconsin

Marshall Erdman, the late founder and developer of Middleton Hills, delighted in calling his new development "an experiment." Indeed, for Middleton, a suburb of Madison, Wisconsin, the new project's tightly spaced, close-to-the-street houses are a substantial departure from the large-lot, developer-built subdivisions typical of the area. Initially viewed as something of a curiosity by Middleton residents and home-builders alike, the traditional neighborhood development (TND) is now beginning to take off; the first crop of residents report great satisfaction with their new neighborhood.

To date, 111 residences have been completed or are under construction, including 45 single-family detached houses, seven townhouses, four live/work units, and a 55-unit condominium building for seniors. In addition, two retail office buildings, totaling 20,000 square feet, have been completed in the commercial district. Inspired by the regional influence of Frank Lloyd Wright, and codified in the community's neighborhood code, much of the construction at Middleton Hills has been designed in the prairie style of architecture.

The master plan for Middleton Hills is being implemented in phases, as demand for lots warrants. Streets and infrastructure for three of the planned six phases have been constructed to date. Of the 45 single-family detached units now completed, 30 have been built by owner-users, 13 have been constructed on spec by local builders, and two have been built speculatively by Marshall Erdman & Associates. Marshall Erdman & Associates also designed and built the commercial buildings and the live/work units.

The land for Middleton Hills—160 acres of wooded hills and wetlands—had been in the Erdman family for some 30 years, with the town of Middleton all the while growing around it. By the early 1990s, Erdman—an architect, developer, and former student of Frank Lloyd Wright—was asked by the mayor of Middleton to either sell or develop the land for needed housing. Not wanting to build "just another subdivision," Erdman turned to new urbanist Andres Duany, of Duany Plater-Zyberk & Company, to plan and design a new order of community, one that would both preserve the natural features of the site and establish a unique sense of identity and community.

The site for Middleton Hills has been called by Duany a "lucky site" for its wealth of natural features: within the site's borders are stands of mature native oaks and black cherry trees; hillsides with views as far as the state capitol dome eight miles away; and rich wetlands that have been preserved and enhanced with native vegetation. The master plan for Middleton Hills is woven around these critical

Marshall Erdman & Associates

1

A row of single-family houses in Middleton Hills.

2

Narrow streets and setbacks, but wide planting strips, define the community's character. A comfortable intimacy is created that will be further enhanced as trees grow to form a canopy over sidewalks.

3

The master plan for Middleton Hills was developed with consideration for critical natural areas and view corridors overlaid with provisions for pedestrian mobility. Interconnected streets disperse traffic flow evenly rather than funnel it onto collector roads as in the typical suburban model.

Marshall Erdman & Associates

4

open spaces and view corridors and tied to them through a series of landscape easements and planned walkways. About one-quarter of the site has been set aside for preservation and recreation.

A mixed-use neighborhood center occupies the flat terrain adjacent to the project's main entry. Small shops with offices or residences above are planned to line the curving streets. The first commercial building constructed contains a neighborhood convenience store and coffee bar, as well as a sales office for the project. By design, mail for Middleton Hills residents is delivered to this central location to encourage interaction among residents. A broad plaza dotted with tables and umbrellas fronts the building, providing an appealing spot to sit and chat or drink coffee.

The emphasis in the neighborhood center design is on pedestrian circulation. With the exception of the signature building now completed, the intention is for shopfronts to hug the curving streets, encouraging strolling and socializing. Parking will be provided behind the shops, with passages between groups of buildings for pedestrian access.

Capitalizing on the topography, the master plan allocates four sites for civic structures: potentially a school, a nature center, a museum or library, and other community buildings. The chosen sites occupy high ground or are otherwise prominent, and they provide focal points for the organization of the project's residential streets.

Unlike conventional subdivisions, there are no cul-de-sac streets at Middleton Hills. Rather, continuous, interconnected streets are planned, in order to even out traffic flow and avoid the need for major collector roads. Streets are organized into traditional blocks, with alley access to rear-loaded parking. Public streets also provide continuous frontage along the wetlands park, maximizing its accessibility and its public benefit.

Street design was one of the more contentious issues during the subdivision approval process for Middleton Hills. Standard practice, endorsed by the Middleton public works and fire departments, would have required streets that were 36 feet wide. Both the developer and land planner lobbied for a narrower standard, in order to build a more intimate—and arguably safer—community.

The negotiated results are 28-foot-wide two-way streets with parking on one side only; 24-foot-wide two-way streets with no parking; and 20-foot-wide one-way streets with no parking. Although residents love the resultant intimacy of the community, the limited on-street parking is an issue that may be revisited in the future.

Duany Plater-Zyberk & Company

Marshall Erdman & Associates

Streets are narrower, but the pedestrian space between the street and the building lot is wider than the norm. To encourage pedestrian activity, residential front lot lines are set back 13 feet from the curb, allowing for a five-foot sidewalk and an eight-foot planting strip.

Contributing to Middleton Hills's perceived intimacy—and its social nature—is the project's mandatory "build-to" line. From the front property line, houses must be set back no more (and no less) than eight feet in most cases with front porches set forward of this line. Not only is this distance shorter than is typical in Middleton (and in suburbs in general), but the very concept of a build-to line, as opposed to a minimum setback line, conveys the sea change in sensibility about community building that Middleton Hills represents. New urbanist communities around the country represent kindred attitudes.

The vision for Middleton Hills—and the regulations to ensure its realization—are detailed in the Middleton Hills neighborhood code. The code's "urban regulations" are essentially the zoning requirements, and they work in concert with the regulating plan, a

4, 5

Middleton Hills encourages front porches for both social and aesthetic reasons. The outdoor space at the front of the house becomes more usable and encourages interaction among neighbors; the rhythm of the streetscape is maintained despite different architectural styles and building materials.

6

Most garages are accessed via privately maintained rear alleys. Unlike garages in some earlier new urbanist communities, some garages are attached to the house, a major advantage in Wisconsin's climate.

7

kind of zoning map. Each lot is coded on the regulating plan as one of six lot types, ranging from "cottages" on 32-foot- and 48-foot-wide lots to "houses" on 64-foot and 80-foot lots. Other lot types provide for townhouses, live/work units, courtyard apartments, and shopfront/lofts. Each lot type, in turn, has regulations specifying permissible building use, building placement on the lot, permissible encroachments, parking, and building height. The intent is to allow for individuality of houses but also to ensure that the ensemble has a visual coherence and supports the overall design concept for the project.

The code's architectural regulations govern the style of houses that may be built. Three styles are permitted: prairie, craftsman, and bungalow. In all three styles, single-family homes must have raised front entrances—a minimum of two feet above grade. Front porches are encouraged, and are required on houses set on wider lots—those 64 and 80 feet wide. Detailed regulations governing base elements (foundations), middle elements (walls and glazing), and roof elements steer designers toward the correct design vocabulary, materials, and proportions, and the mandatory design review of each structure provides the enforcement lever. To avoid land speculation, the neighborhood code requires construction of houses to be completed no later than 15 months after lot purchase.

Garages at Middleton Hills are required, in most instances, to be located at the rear of the lot, accessed from alleys. They may be separate structures or attached to the main residence. The alleys, which are 30 feet wide (14 feet paved), are privately owned and maintained, unlike the streets, which are dedicated to the city. Accessory dwelling units are encouraged by the neighborhood code to be constructed over garages—but to date, only a few have been built.

Currently, the design review board is controlled by the developer, and design reviews are principally carried out by the project's design director, Jane Grabowski-Miller, an employee of the developer. According to the project covenants, however, control of the design review board ultimately will pass to the Middleton Hills neighborhood association.

The reaction to Middleton Hills has been varied. Initially, the project generated intense interest, according to Paul Brunsell, project director for Middleton Hills, but the early interest was tempered by the lack of model homes and a negative perception of the density of the initial homes, which were built by private lot owners. Builders were reluctant to build on speculation because of the novelty of the concept and the code requirements and because of the uncertain market expectations for the project. And finally, given that prospective residents have to persevere through a typically year-long design/build process, due to the custom-designed houses, the project has taken time to mature. However, when enough

Duany Plater-Zyberk & Company

9

Marshall Erdman & Associates

8

7, 8

Three architectural styles, each based on the local vernacular of the early 20th century, are permitted by the code: bungalow, craftsman, and Frank Lloyd Wright–inspired prairie style.

9

Aerial perspective of Middleton Hills showing sites reserved for civic buildings.

homes were built to give buyers a more accurate picture of the concept, the rate of lot sales began increasing, and speculatively built houses are now selling as quickly as they come to market. "There is a sense of neighborhood character that people want," Grabowski-Miller comments, and Madison-area residents increasingly are looking to Middleton Hills to satisfy that desire.

case study

Middleton Hills

Middleton Hills, Wisconsin

land use information

Site Area:	160 acres
Total Dwelling Units:	635[1]
Gross Project Density:	4.0 units per acre
Housing Types:	Single-family, townhouses, live/work, apartments
Average Lot Size:	4,000 square feet (single-family)
Gross Residential Density:	6.3 units per acre
Project Completion Date:	Being built in phases

land use plan

	Acres	Percent of Site
Residential	80[1]	50.0%
Recreation/Amenities	20[1]	12.5%
Roads/Parking	20[1]	12.5%
Open Space	20[1]	12.5%
Other (commercial)	20[1]	12.5%
Total	160	100.0%

[1]Estimates: subject to change.

Duany Plater-Zyberk & Company

10

10, 11

Street elevations.

12

The first commercial building in Middleton Hills has first-floor retail with office space above. It includes the sales office for the project, a convenience store, and a coffee bar with outdoor tables along the sidewalk.

12

Marshall Erdman & Associates

Duany Plater-Zyberk & Company

11

unit information

Unit Type	Lot Size (Square Feet)	Floor Area (Square Feet)	Number Planned/ Built	Current Sales Prices
Single-family detached	2,800–8,800	900–3,900	325/45	$140,000–$390,000
Townhouse	N/A	1,643–1,818	30/7	$199,000+
Live/work	N/A	2,000	30/4	$214,500
Multifamily (1- and 2-bdrm)	N/A	N/A	250/55	$27,000–$68,000
Total			635/111	

contact information

Developer	Middleton Hills, Inc. Marshall Erdman & Associates 5117 University Avenue Madison, Wisconsin 53705 608-238-0211
Town Planner	Duany Plater-Zyberk & Company 1023 Southwest 25th Avenue Miami, Florida 33135 305-644-1023

case study

Amberleigh

Mill Creek, Washington

At first glance, Amberleigh appears to be a neighborhood of modest—but appealing—single-family detached homes in a range of styles. One sees a Tudor bungalow, then a Cape Cod, then a craftsman; one home in shades of green, another in tones of mauve. In fact, however, Amberleigh is a subdivision of duplexes and fourplexes, artfully arranged in such a way that common walls are recessed and concealed and garages for the quad units are grouped into parking courts, hidden from view. Designed by Mithun Partners, Inc., the 88-unit project achieves its single-family look with a net density of 7.6 units per acre.

The Amberleigh site is a sloping 15-acre parcel located in Mill Creek, a mostly large-lot, single-family suburb of Seattle, Washington. The site was one of the few remaining undevel-

Note: Images for this case study are courtesy of Mithun Partners.

1

oped parcels in a popular master-planned community; as such, it came with a relatively high price tag. Market studies by the developer, however, established a firm ceiling on achievable sales prices, implying the necessity of increased densities. At the same time, under Washington State's growth management policies, Mill Creek, which falls within Seattle's urban growth boundary, was under pressure to increase the density in new residential development. The challenge, then, was to design an attached housing project that retained the appeal of a single-family detached neighborhood. As Bill Kreager, principal of Mithun Partners, characterizes the dilemma: "If it looks dense, potential buyers will stay in their cars."

The design concept that emerged revolves around two issues: maximizing a unique appearance for each dwelling unit, and minimizing the visual impact of the automobile. To promote the single-family look and feel of the project, the major two-story portion of each dwelling is pushed forward, close to the street, while the one-story remainder of the house (or garage, in the case of the duplexes) is recessed. The effect, seen in oblique perspective, is a rhythm of two-story volumes that read as individual houses. Further

1

Amberleigh's 15-acre site includes 88 attached units, a community park, and three acres of naturalized landscaped buffer around the project.

2, 3

Increasing density while maintaining the community's single-family character was the goal at Amberleigh. What appears to be a row of single-family houses of regional architectural styles is actually a series of duplexes and fourplexes, each attached at the garage. Rear parking courts and garages reached by common driveways keep the streetscape attractive and hold curb cuts to a minimum. The parking treatment visually enhances the streetscape and improves pedestrian safety.

accentuating the individuality of units is the random assignment of styles and colors, intended to recall the charm of old Seattle. "Architectural character," comments Kreager, "is a key to minimizing the perceived density."

Also contributing to the traditional character of the project is the relative lack of curb cuts and street-fronting garages for the fourplex units. Typically, one curb cut is provided for every four dwelling units. A landscaped 12-foot-wide driveway leads back to a 44-foot by 64-foot parking court, which serves the two-car garages of each of the four attached dwelling units and provides two additional apron parking spaces per unit. Most of the garages are not visible from the street.

A three-acre area protecting native plants rings the Amberleigh site on three sides. Typically 50 feet wide, the protection zone includes a variety of indigenous shrub and tree species, including evergreen firs and cedars, alders, and maples. While protecting some of the Northwest's rapidly diminishing native flora, the zone also serves to shield the residences from adjacent traffic and development.

Once inside the project, one sees a half-acre community park, the focus of community events, block parties, and holiday celebrations. Residences look out on the park as they might on a traditional village green.

Residential lot sizes average 5,000 square feet. Quad lots are almost square, measuring approximately 58 feet by 74 feet. Dwelling units are typically set back just 11 feet from

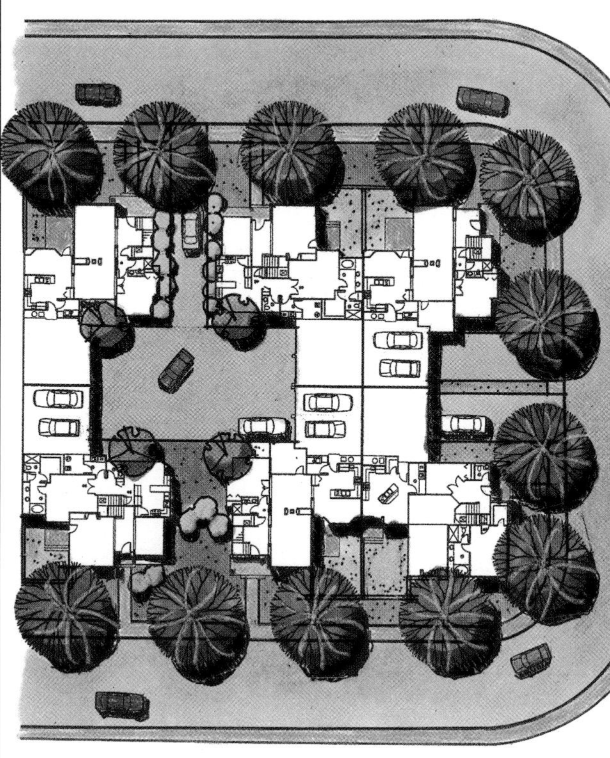

4

A half-acre common area provides space for a landscaped community park. In addition, a 50-foot-wide band of natural growth surrounds the project on three sides.

5

Plan of typical fourplex showing attached garages and parking courts.

6

When garages face the street, they are pushed back to minimize their visual impact. Each home has a two-car garage plus space for two additional off-street parking spaces. Exteriors are offered in a range of styles, unified by such materials as cedar shake roofing, and stone, wood, and shingle siding.

the sidewalk, or 15 feet from the curb. In addition to the more public front yard landscaping, open to the street, each unit has a small enclosed patio, usually tucked into the recess of the single-story portion of the residence. The landscape visible from the public areas is maintained by a homeowners' association.

Five unit floor plans were offered at Amberleigh, ranging in size from a 1,457-square-foot two-bedroom/den unit to a 2,192-square-foot three-bedroom model. In four of the five models, the master bedroom suite is on the first floor, a preference of the targeted empty nester market. A loft with one or two bedrooms is located upstairs. With the exception of some cathedral ceilings, ceiling heights are nine feet, now standard in medium-priced developments in this market.

Sales at Amberleigh averaged about four per month. True to the initial market study, buyers were predominantly empty nesters, with a small portion of them younger singles and couples without children. Initially, homes were priced at $205,000 to $244,500. By the conclusion of sales, prices reached $300,000 for the largest units.

In an era of mandatory state growth management regulations, limited land availability, and spiraling land costs, Amberleigh presents a successful model for suburban infill housing development. In fact, the Amberleigh fourplex design is now being built in several locations around the country, including Atlanta, Georgia; Lafayette, Indiana; and Illinois. Through its innovative site planning, architectural massing and detail, as well as landscape design, Amberleigh succeeds as "housing that doesn't feel dense"—architect Kreager's first goal—and yet exceeds the norm for suburban housing.

6

case study

amberleigh

mill creek, washington

7

land use information

Site Area:	15.16 acres
Total Dwelling Units:	88
Gross Project Density:	5.8 units per acre (Including native-growth protection easements and village green)
Housing Types:	Duplex, fourplex
Average Lot Size:	+/– 5,000 square feet
Gross Residential Density:	7.6 units per acre
Parking, Total:	352 spaces (plus on-street parking)
Parking Ratio:	4 spaces/unit (plus on-street parking)
Project Completion Date:	Fall 1998

land use plan

	Acres	Percentage of Site
Residential	10.10	66.7%
Recreation/Amenities	0.50	3.3%
Roads/Parking	1.52	10.0%
Open Space	3.04	20.0%
Total	15.16	100.0%

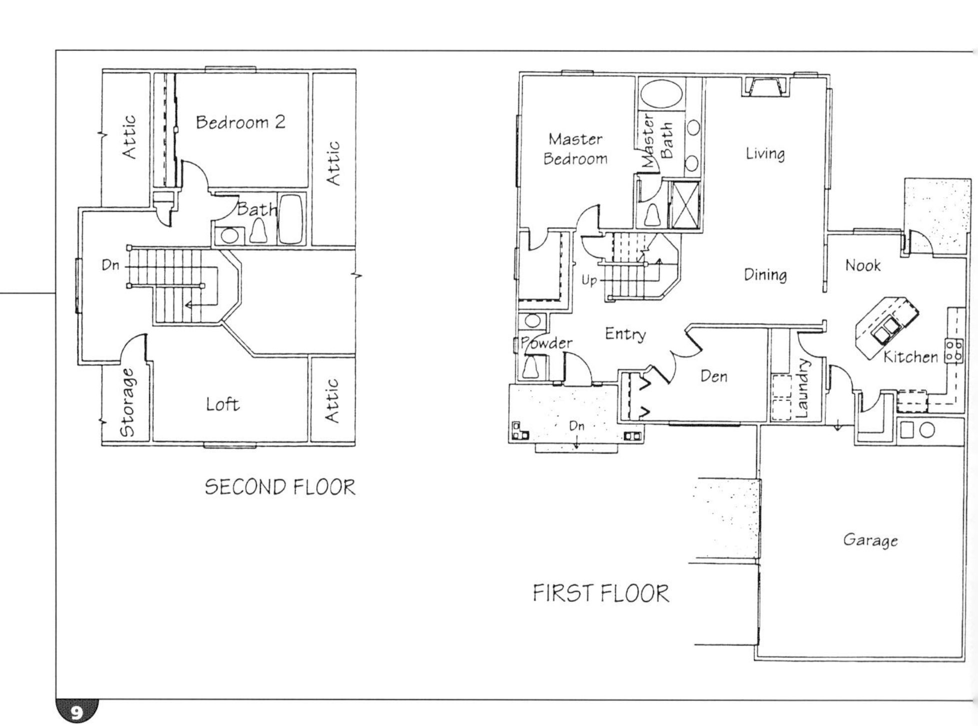

9

7, 8

Even from the rear, the project gives the impression of being a single-family community. Shared driveways and parking courts help to minimize the paved area.

9

Typical unit floor plan.

contact information

Developer	William E. Buchan Homes 11555 Northup Way Bellevue, Washington 98004 425-828-6424
Architect and Land Planner	Mithun Partners, Inc. 414 Olive Way, #500 Seattle, Washington 98101 206-623-3344
Landscape Architect	Williamson Landscape Architecture, LLC 1737 Northwest 56th Street, #101 Seattle, Washington 98107 206-784-7996

development costs

	Total	Cost per Dwelling Unit	Cost per Residential Square Foot
Site Acquisition Cost	$1,714,000	$19,477	$10.49
Site Improvement Cost	$3,101,989	$35,250	$18.98
Construction Cost	$12,691,977	$144,227	$77.67
Soft Costs	$2,088,972	$23,738	$12.78
Total Cost	$19,596,938	$222,692	$119.92

unit information

Unit Type	Lot Size (Square Feet)	Floor Area (Square Feet)	Number Planned/ Built	Final Sales Prices or Rent
2-bdrm + loft/2 1/2-bath	5,200	1,790	16/16	$225,500
2-bdrm/2 1/2-bath	4,800	1,882	22/22	$252,500
2-bdrm/2-bath	5,000	1,451	12/12	$262,500
3-bdrm/2 1/2-bath	5,000	1,656	21/21	$265,500
3-bdrm + loft/2 1/2-bath	5,000	2,192	20/20	$285,900

8

case study

Harbor Town

Memphis, Tennessee

Harbor Town turned ten years old in 1999, making it one of the older—and one of the most successful—of the crop of new urbanist communities. The 135-acre project is located on Mud Island, virtually in the shadow of downtown Memphis. Now mostly built out, Harbor Town evokes the traditional town: gridded streets, a strong pedestrian orientation, formally planned squares, and architectural forms based on historical prototypes. And like many older towns, there is a successful mix of housing types; at Harbor Town one can find $800-per-month rentals just a few steps from $800,000 riverfront homes.

After a decade, 818 of the planned 875 dwelling units are now completed. About half of the units built are for-sale housing (mostly single-family detached units). The remainder are rental apartments. A Montessori school; a 50-slip marina; and a mixed-use town center containing shops, services, and a 6,500-square-foot grocery store also have been constructed. A yacht club and office building (with a combined size of 53,500 square feet) along with high-end condominiums are expected to finish out the town center by the end of 1999.

Harbor Town is the vision of developer Henry Turley. Turley already had a reputation as an imaginative Memphis-based developer when, in the late 1980s, he saw an opportunity to build a new downtown community, one that would be much like the Memphis neighborhood where he grew up. Turley recalls, "Right there in my neighborhood, there seemed to be everything—a hint of all of life's possibilities mixed with all kinds of people." Turley sought to recreate this neighborhood ethos, and the sense of community it engendered, in Harbor Town.

The site of Harbor Town—Mud Island—was created early in the 20th century by a natural buildup of sand along the eastern bank of the Mississippi River. During the 1960s, the island was raised above the 100-year floodplain through dredging operations by the U.S. Army Corps of Engineers. The island remained largely undeveloped, however, until a bridge was built connecting it with downtown Memphis in the mid-1980s. Developer Turley and his partners acquired the Harbor Town site in 1987.

Note: Images for this case study are courtesy of Looney Ricks Kiss Architects, Inc.

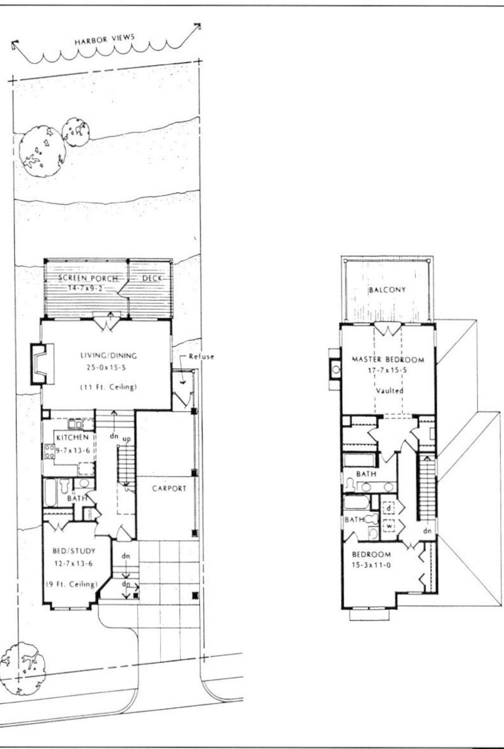

HARBOR TOWN PLANNED DEVELOPMENT
ISLAND PROPERTIES ASSOCIATES
MEMPHIS, TENNESSEE

1, 3

Harbor Town's smallest houses are among its more interesting examples. Traditional southern shotgun houses and two-story cottages serve as models for single-family homes on 25- to 30-foot-wide lots. While the form is traditional, the interpretation is contemporary.

2

Harbor Town's 135-acre plan occupies a portion of Mud Island, just across the Mississippi River from downtown Memphis. A town center includes community shopping and services.

4

Floor plan for two-story cottages.

5

The plan for Harbor Town, designed by RTKL Associates, is composed of a series of radial boulevards superimposed on a grid of blocks. The radials serve to open the interior of the site to views of the Mississippi River and the downtown skyline. Neighborhood parks terminate the radial boulevards and other major streets and provide a visual and psychological focus for the individual neighborhoods within Harbor Town. A wetlands detention feature running through the center of the site is designed to look like a stream and ponds, creating a naturalistic but distinct edge between neighborhoods. A 1.2-mile-long nature/jogging trail runs through the park, which also includes several seating areas. The town center, located toward the southern edge of the community, continues the formal system of radials and focal points.

While the original master plan divided each block into 50-foot-wide lots with front-access driveways, the plan was subsequently amended to provide for rear-access alleys and the diversification of lot widths. Lots as narrow as 25 feet were created for the smallest detached homes. According to town architect J. Carson Looney, who devised the alley/small-lot retrofit scheme, "We created a variety of lot sizes in order to capture an unserved and important market segment. It was critical to diversify unit types and prices on the interior lots located away from the river and with fewer amenities."

With the intent of creating a more intimate and pedestrian-scaled community, local streets at Harbor Town are narrow and short, and building setbacks are minimized. Local street rights-of-way are 44 feet wide, with a 28-foot curb-to-curb distance, including parking on both sides of the street. The traffic-calming effect is evident: "It is difficult to drive more than 15 miles an hour almost anywhere in the community," Looney notes. During the approval process, the city refused to accept ownership of the narrow streets, requiring Harbor Town's streets to be private. However, after years of proof that such streets create a more livable environment, Harbor Town's standards have become a model for public streets elsewhere in Memphis.

Single-family residential setbacks are typically 10 to 15 feet from the property line. Garages, in most instances, are kept off the street, accessed via rear alleyways that were established as easements carved out of adjoining properties. Where parking is accessed directly from the street, garages are set back—and in some cases covered by second-story porches —to minimize their visual impact.

Construction of Harbor Town began in 1989. During the first phase, the developer discovered that written design standards were difficult for designers, builders, and buyers to understand. To counter this, Looney Ricks Kiss Architects (LRK) established a set of visual design guidelines that implemented developer Turley's vision in an easy-to-understand format of "do's" and "don'ts." The visual guidelines do not prescribe any particular architectural style, but they do set the basic ground rules for street facades, scale and proportion, materials, and key details. In support of the traditional architectural vernacular, the guidelines require, for example, that windows be oriented vertically, rather than horizontally, and that porches be raised 24 to 30 inches above grade. In addition to establishing an overall aesthetic for the community, the intent of the design guidelines is to ensure that lower-priced homes on narrow lots maintain a level of design compatible in quality to the more expensive homes—a key to successful sales price mixing, according to architect Looney.

5

Harbor Town's neotraditional plan incorporates a series of radial boulevards over a grid of streets.

6

The rhythm of repeating classical forms unifies the streetscape.

7

While 12 different architects have designed houses for some 20 different builders, LRK has designed about 65 percent of the single-family units and townhouses at Harbor Town. Most of the residential designs are updates of local vernacular forms, ranging from Charleston side-yard homes to simple shotgun cottages, although some units are more modern in detail.

The small-lot designs by LRK are among the most interesting and innovative. Situated on lots as small as 25 to 30 feet by 100 to 110 feet, these dwelling units typically are side-yard designs, one room wide (occasionally two), with alley garages. In many instances, the units have raised front porches and second-story balconies to engage the street. In some designs, the porches wrap around to the side yard, creating a sheltered extension to the outdoors. The yards themselves are effectively laid out, with patios and courts, all with an eye toward maintaining privacy. Architectural details, such as eight-foot-high doors and 10-foot-high ceilings, are used to offset the small footprints and give the units a sense of spaciousness that belies the actual numbers.

The appeal of the small-lot housing also is facilitated by LRK's subdivision design. By orienting the smaller lots toward neighborhood parks, the units in essence borrow the communal open space. Although lacking in river views, lots fronting the neighborhood parks sold quickly and commanded premium prices.

Initially, Harbor Town was a hard sell to builders and buyers alike. New growth was occurring on the eastern side of the metropolitan area—and certainly not adjacent to downtown. Considerable effort and expense were required to persuade builders to construct houses speculatively and to persuade realtors to bring prospective buyers to see them. Expecting that sales to families would be among the most difficult to close—given the local school choices available—developer Turley initially offered lot price concessions of $1,200 per child. Also, an on-site Montessori school was organized; it now has been expanded twice.

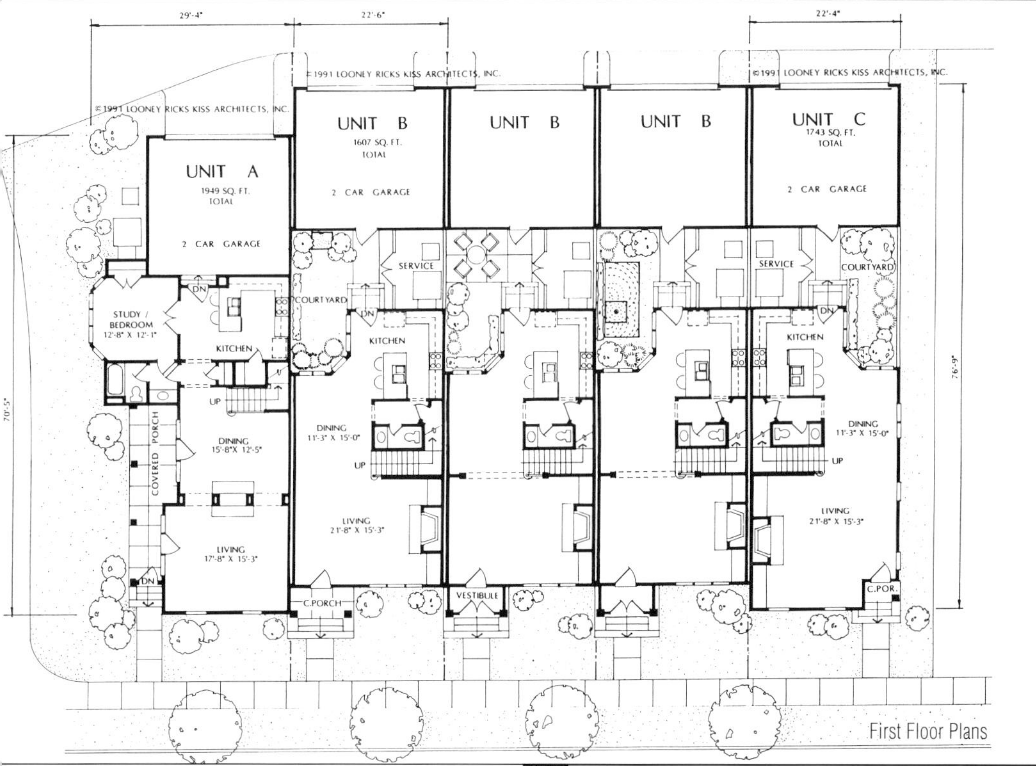

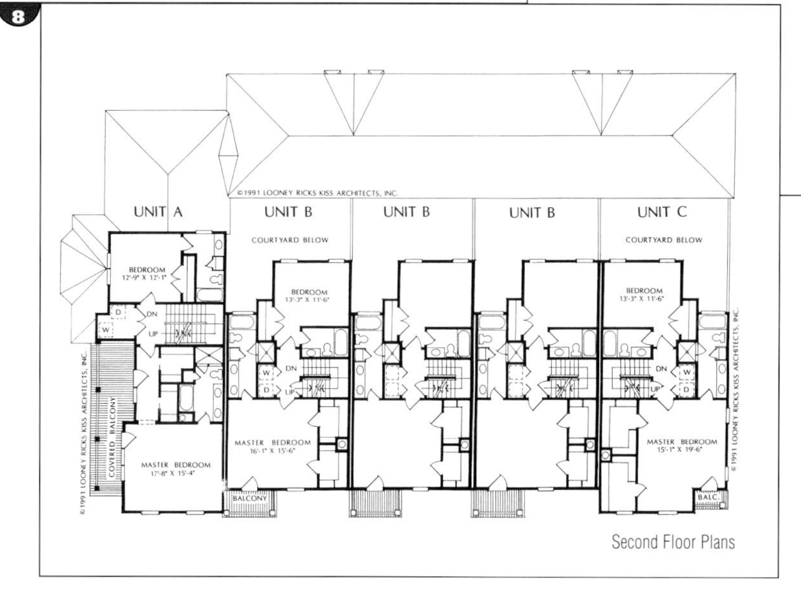

7

A row of townhouses, given a classic southern colonial treatment, has the appearance of a large single-family house. Each unit includes a detached two-car garage and private outdoor courtyard or covered side porch.

8

Rowhouse plans for first and second floors.

9

Harbor Town's plan and code allow for a wide variety of housing, from rental apartments to custom homes. Traditional southern styles through clean-lined contemporary styles all are at home in the community's mix of architecture.

Through these efforts, and through the design of the community itself—everything from front porches to neighborhood parks—Harbor Town has been able to win over a substantial number of families with children. Overall, given the wide variety of housing sizes and prices offered, the project has attracted a wide spectrum of buyers, including empty nesters, singles, and professional couples, as well as families. Similarly, under the umbrella of the community's design guidelines, Harbor Town has been able to integrate a mixture of custom homes, plan-book homes, and production housing.

As Harbor Town enters the last stages of its buildout, there is empirical evidence that the homebuying public recognizes its special design qualities. In a 1999 publication by the Urban Land Institute, *Valuing the New Urbanism*, researchers report that Harbor Town has achieved a 25 percent price premium relative to other housing in its market, attributable to the community's design.

In summarizing his vision, Henry Turley philosophizes: "What a neighborhood should do is take the world—or at least a slice of it, the more complete and varied the better—and make it just our size. A place where life with our neighbors can be rich and meaningful and significant, where they know our names." That is a lot to ask for, but it would appear that Harbor Town has gone further toward that goal than most.

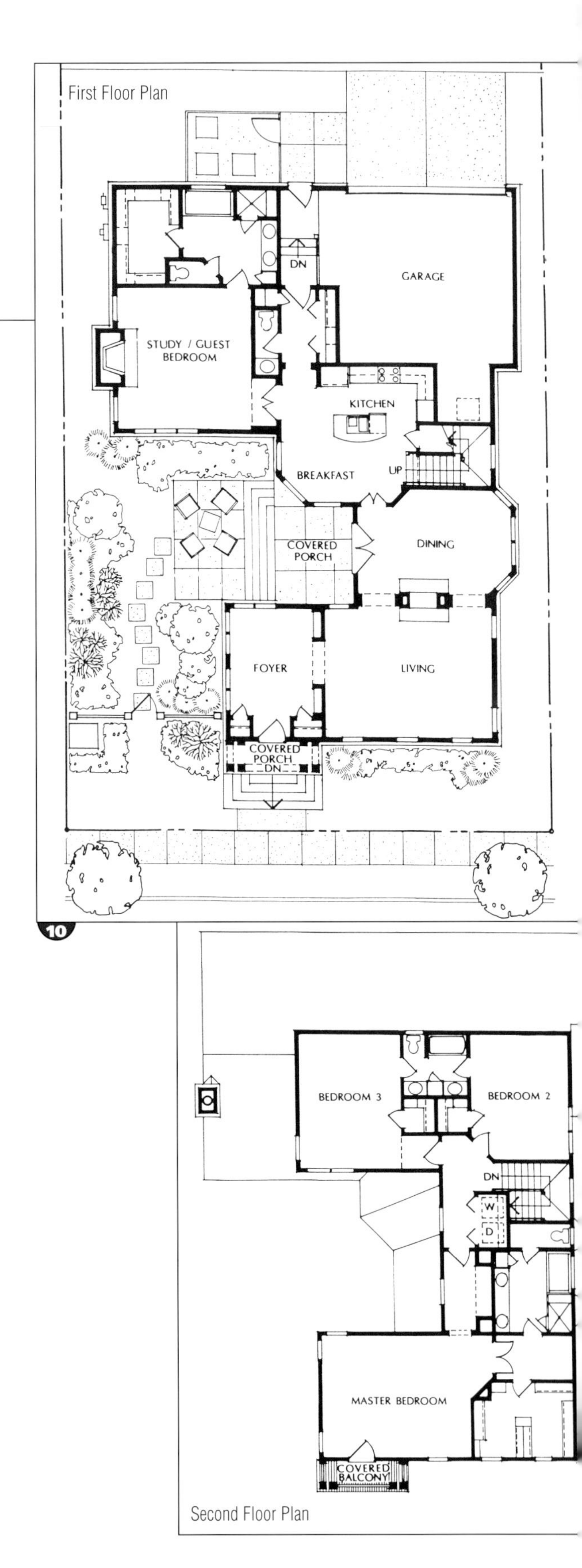

10

First and second floor plans.

11

Behind a traditional facade, an open floor plan for today's lifestyles includes a first-floor guest suite, an attached two-car garage, and a private outdoor courtyard. Elegant proportions and detailing are evident throughout Harbor Town. All housing conforms to the design guidelines, which—rather than dictating a specific architectural style—establish scale, materials, and unifying elements.

case study

Harbortown

Memphis, Tennessee

Land use information

Site Area:	135 gross acres
Total Dwelling Units:	875
Gross Project Density:	6.48 units per acre
Housing Types:	Single-family detached, townhouses, apartments, condominiums
Lot Size:	2,500–7,000 square fet
Gross Residential Density:	9.6 units per acre
Parking Total:	1,750 spaces
Parking Ratio:	2 spaces/unit (plus on-street parking)
Project Completion Date:	2000

Land use plan

	Acres	Percent of Site
Residential	70.5	52.22%
Recreation/Amenities	9.0	6.70%
Roads/Parking	21.0	15.55%
Open Space	27.0	20.03%
Other	7.5	5.52%
Total	135.0	100.00%

12

Harbor Crest Row Houses represent another use of 30-foot lots. The houses make use of high ceilings and tall windows to give the impression of more space. Covered side porches, inspired by traditional homes of the region, provide private outdoor living space on two levels.

13

As is common in new urbanist communities, most garages are at the rear of houses and are reached by alleys.

13

development costs

	Total	Cost per Dwelling Unit
Site Acquisition Cost	$2,251,470	$2,573
Site Improvement Cost	$1,750,000	$2,000
Construction Cost	$6,550,000	$7,486
Soft Costs	$5,500,000	$6,285
Total Cost	$16,051,470	$18,344

unit information

Unit Type	Floor Area (Square Feet)	Number Planned/ Built	Current Sales Prices or Rent
Single-family	1,300–6,500	396/351	$115,000–$1,000,000
Townhouses	1,200–1,700	35/35	$120,000–$180,000
Apartments	630–1,500	420/420	$550–$1,200
Condominiums	1,200–2,400	24/12	$250,000–$350,000
Total		875/818	

contact information

Developer	Henry Turley Company 65 Union Avenue, Suite 1200 Memphis, Tennessee 38103 901-527-2770
Land Planner	RTKL 409 East Pratt Baltimore, Maryland 21022 301-528-8600
Architect and Land Planner	Looney Ricks Kiss Architects, Inc. 88 Union Avenue, Suite 900 Memphis, Tennessee 38103 901-521-1440
Landscape Architect	John Phillips, ASLA Reaves & Sweeney 5118 Poplar Avenue, Suite 400 Memphis, Tennessee 38117 901-761-2016

case study

orenco station

Hillsboro, oregon

"The ability to walk to a quart of milk" is how Rudy Kadlub of Costa Pacific Homes summarizes the philosophy behind the development of Orenco Station, a 190-acre new community in the western suburbs of Portland, Oregon. As the phrase implies, Orenco Station is a pedestrian-oriented, mixed-use community. It was planned by master developer Pacific Realty Associates, LP (PacTrust) for 1,834

1

Ed Hershberger

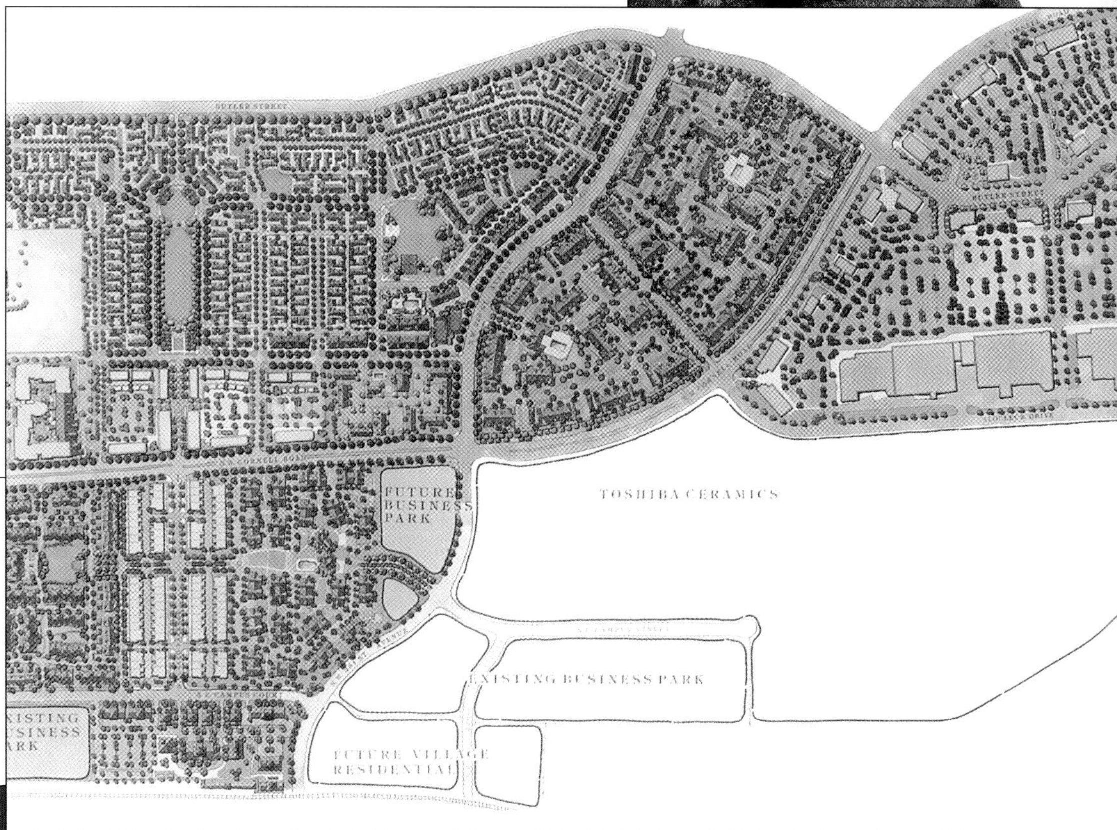

2

Ed Hershberger

1, 2

Orenco Station's compact plan occupies a 190-acre site. The density of the pedestrian-oriented community is mitigated by a system of neighborhood parks.

3

A town center includes neighborhood-oriented shopping and services, while a retail center provides space for larger retailers. Both centers, as well as the transit station, are within walking distance for most residents.

housing units, as well as for retail and office space. The compact design includes a wide range of housing types, from single-family detached houses to accessory units built over garages, to live/work lofts and residences over retail shops. The common thread of the community is a formal system of open spaces and miniparks—a "string of pearls," as the development team calls it—terminating in the recently opened Orenco Station stop of the Tri-Met MAX light rail line, which connects downtown Portland to its suburbs.

Originally zoned for industrial use, and later rezoned for subdivision housing, the present community of Orenco Station was born when the site was designed as a "town center" in the Portland Metro Area 2040 Plan. The plan established a gradient of residential density targets at varying distances from the Orenco light rail stop and mandated mixed-use development. With little precedent for either higher density or mixed-use development in the area, PacTrust, under the direction of CEO Peter Bechen and corporate architect Ken Grimes, assembled a team of designers, engineers, and a homebuilder to explore the locally uncharted waters.

As part of the exploration, market research was conducted among workers in the surrounding high-tech facilities to establish design and housing preferences and to define affordability issues. The survey and subsequent focus group research revealed an attraction to the look and feel of the older Portland suburbs, with their craftsman and cottage architecture, picturesque rose gardens, and neighborhood-oriented shops. The research reflected a somewhat nostalgic outlook, but one that fit well with the concept of a more densely developed—but livable—transit-oriented

Ed Hershberger

Ed Hershberger

development. Two years of discussions, design studies, and negotiations with city, state, and transit officials ensued, culminating in a custom-tailored zoning ordinance for Orenco Station. Dubbed a "station community residential village," or SCRV district, the new zoning established design guidelines that would allow for—and ensure—the sort of heterogeneous and urban mixing of housing types and land uses not typically found in the suburbs.

The light rail station, located at the southern edge of the Orenco Station, is the generative element of the community's site design. The primary circulation network—both vehicular and pedestrian—runs axially from the station to the town center and culminates in a formal village green. Secondary circulation and open spaces branch laterally from this ceremonial spine. The open space and circulation framework have a processional quality, meant to induce a sense of place and a sense of community. Vistas are terminated by strong visual elements, such as the classically inspired pergolas at each end of the village green. By these means, and by the judicious placement of smaller miniparks, the developer and architects have scripted a plan intended to encourage walking—and, on a more philosophical plane, to encourage a more community-oriented way of life.

The town center lies at the intersection of the station's north/south axis and Cornell Road, an existing major arterial road that bisects Orenco Station. The town center structures, designed by Fletcher Farr Ayotte Architects, provide space for small neighborhood retail uses, including a coffee shop and brewpub. Set to open in summer 1999, the retail buildings in some cases will have roll-up door fronts, to allow for outdoor dining along the extra-wide 17-foot sidewalks. Office space and housing will be located on the second and third floors, above the retail uses.

In the residential areas, several design devices were employed to reinforce the pedestrian and community orientation of Orenco Station. Residential street widths were minimized (25 feet, with parking on one side), and sidewalks are bulbed as a way to narrow intersections and slow traffic. To further reduce the impact of the automobile, Orenco's site design provides alley ("drive lane") parking access, thereby eliminating the usual garage-door-dominated front building elevations and ubiquitous curb cuts and driveways. To minimize costs, drive-lane paving was held to a width of 16 feet, with turn-ins expanding to the full 24 feet from garage face to garage face. The space between the garage turn-ins is used for plantings, which soften the drive-lane appearance.

Single-family lots at Orenco Station are relatively small, ranging from 3,680 to 4,500 square feet. The smallest lots are typically 40 feet wide. Dwelling units are positioned five feet from the side lot line on one side, with an easement to use the five-foot yard granted to the abutting lot. The net result, incorporating the adjacent property's "passive-use" easement, is a usable side yard 12 to 15 feet wide (in a

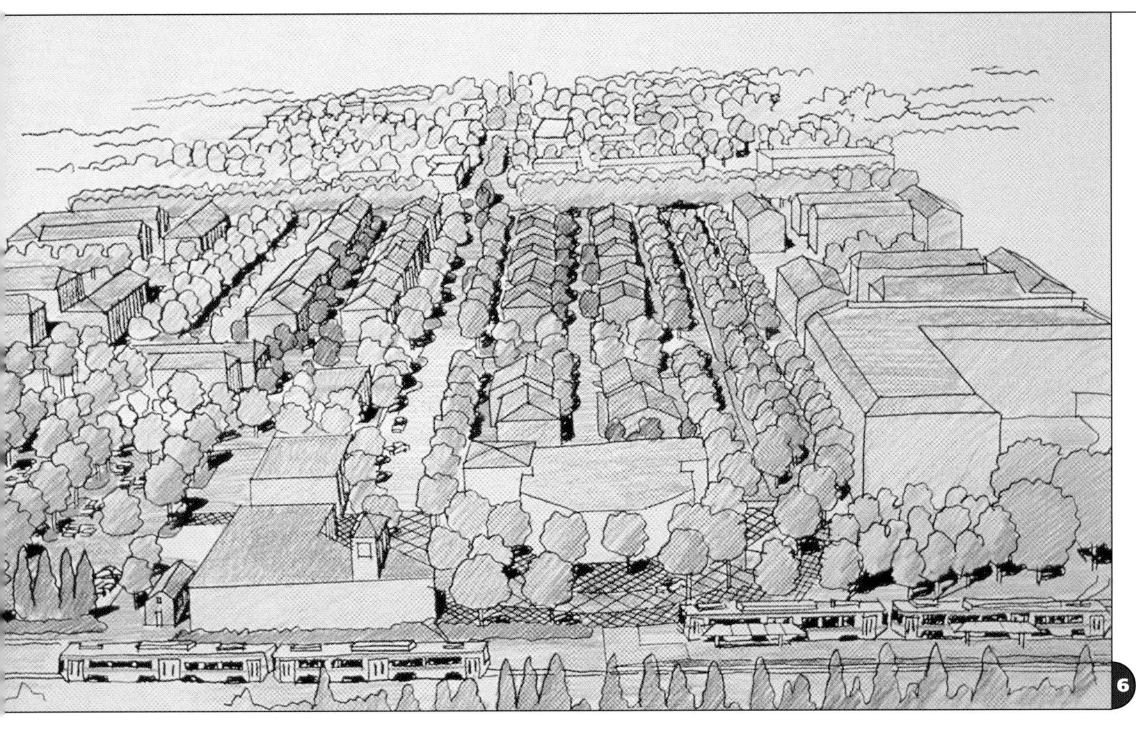

4

The town center includes small retail uses on first levels, with offices and housing above. Some of the buildings have roll-up glass door fronts that open to outdoor cafés along the 17-foot-wide sidewalks.

5

The MAX light rail system links Orenco Station to downtown Portland and surrounding areas. Streets and walkways are designed to encourage walking to transit.

6

The master plan includes 1,834 housing units of a variety of types—from live/work lofts to single-family houses.

40-foot-wide lot), running the length of the house. The layout of houses is similar to the more traditional zero-lot-line layout, in which each house's footprint is pushed fully to one side of the lot (a zero-foot setback). The difference is that in a zero-lot-line layout, windows are not permitted by code on the lot line building elevation, and the lot line wall has to be one-hour fire rated. By pushing the unit five feet off the lot line and granting the easement, the Orenco houses net the same side yard as a zero-lot-line unit but have the benefit of windows on the side elevation. Visual intrusion into the neighboring side yard is held to a minimum by placing the windows high in the space.

Orenco's dwelling units are held close to the street with eight-foot maximum setbacks for townhouses and 13-to19-foot setbacks for detached housing units. Facade designs are based on Portland-area craftsman and English cottage precedents, and most have front porches. While the smaller-than-typical front yard setbacks and the front porch elements are intended to encourage a more active and engaged street life, the dwelling units are raised above the sidewalk, as in many older Portland neighborhoods, to afford a measure of privacy.

The issue of accessory units or carriage homes over garages was approached cautiously by the development team, because the market

Ed Hershberger

7, 8

Based on consumer surveys, architectural guidelines were developed to reflect the craftsman and cottage styles prevalent in older Portland suburbs.

9

A two-bedroom cottage floor plan, with optional carriage house unit.

for these spaces, as well as the impact of mixing smaller residential units with the larger main residences, was relatively untested in the market. The 514-square-foot carriage homes were offered as a buyer's option, with two different plan configurations: a studio option (one large room, a bath, and a small closet) and an apartment option (living room, sleeping alcove, kitchen, and bath). About one in three buyers has purchased the accessory space; most of these have taken the apartment version, currently priced at $49,500.

Use of the added space has been varied; some owners have used it as office space or as a guest suite, and others have rented it as an apartment. The accessory units have separate legal addresses and are entered directly from the drive lanes via an exterior stair. One parking space is carved out of the rear portion of the lot for each accessory unit. The dwelling units have windows that overlook the drive lane. They also have a small porch at the top of the stairs, which provides a measure of activity and oversight for the drive lanes.

Orenco's housing units are relatively small: single-family detached models range from 1,400 to 1,700 square feet. Unit designs include two- and three-bedroom models, although some models have flexible spaces allowing for conversion to three- or four-bedroom residences. Responding to emerging lifestyle patterns and preferences, all units have a dedicated home office space, typically an alcove or open area off a second-floor stair landing. Dwelling units are constructed with high-speed wiring for computer communication as well.

Unlike more traditional subdivisions, the three- and four-unit townhouse structures are integrated with the single-family detached

Ed Hershberger

housing, often sited at the ends of single-family blocks. As residential architect Lee Iverson puts it, "The townhouses at Orenco Station are not segregated into some sort of townhouse corral." From the exterior, the townhouse structures are designed to look like larger cousins to the adjacent single-family houses, with asymmetric and varied facades and entryways.

Other residences, designed by Fletcher Farr Ayotte Architects, will be located above the retail shops in the town center. FFA also has designed three-story live/work units for the rear parcels of the town center. These units

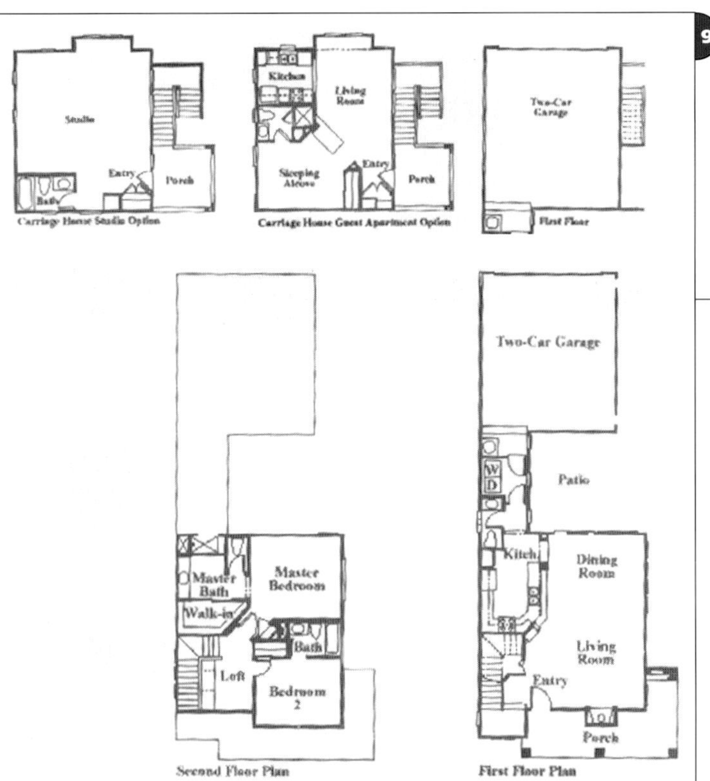

will offer a ground-floor professional office/studio combined with a two-story loft residence.

Sales at Orenco Station have exceeded projections, according to Rudy Kadlub of Costa Pacific Homes. Absorption has averaged 7.5 units per month, and prices are running about 20 to 30 percent above the area average. Demographically, homebuyers at Orenco Station have been primarily singles, professional couples, and empty nesters. As might be expected, because of the small-lot/small-unit design, only a minority of buyers have been families with children.

The experience of Orenco Station has demonstrated that higher densities and mixed housing types can be successful in suburban markets. The success, argues PacTrust and its design team, is due in large measure to the attention paid to the public realm, which offsets the smaller private space offered to buyers. Although the town center is not yet completed, the project's community and pedestrian orientation have been cited in post-purchase focus groups as primary reasons for purchasing a home at Orenco Station.

case study

orenco station

Hillsboro, Oregon

land use information

Site Area:	61.2 acres[1]
Total Dwelling Units:	446
Gross Project Density:	7.3 units per acre
Housing Types:	Single-family detached, townhouses, condominiums
Lot Size:	3,000 square feet
Gross Residential Density:	10.85 units per acre
Parking, Total:	835 spaces
Parking Ratio:	1.9 spaces/unit
Project Completion Date:	2001 (estimated)

[1]Of 190-acre total master plan.

land use plan

	Acres	Percent of Site
Residential	30.2	49.4%
Recreation/Amenities	1.1	1.7%
Roads/Parking	20.1	32.8%
Open Space	7.8	12.7%
Other (mixed use)	2.0	3.3%
Total	61.2	100.0%

contact information

Master Developer	Pacific Realty Associates, LP (PacTrust) 15350 Southwest Sequoia Parkway Suite 300 Portland, Oregon 97224 503-624-6300
Residential Development Partner	Costa Pacific Homes 8625 Southwest Cascade Avenue Suite 606 Beaverton, Oregon 97008 503-646-8888
Residential Architect	Iverson Associates, Inc. 151 Kalmus Drive, C140 Costa Mesa, California 92626 714-549-3479
Town Center Architect	Fletcher Farr Ayotte 708 Southwest Third Street, Suite 200 Portland, Oregon 97204 503-222-1661
Landscape Architect	Walker & Macy 111 Southwest Oak, Suite 200 Portland, Oregon 97204 503-228-3122

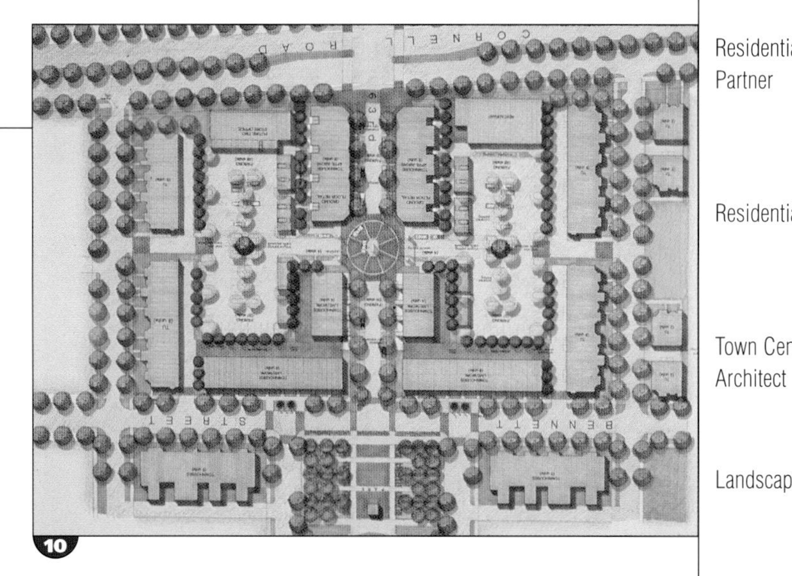
10

10, 11
Town center.

12
Town center loft plan.

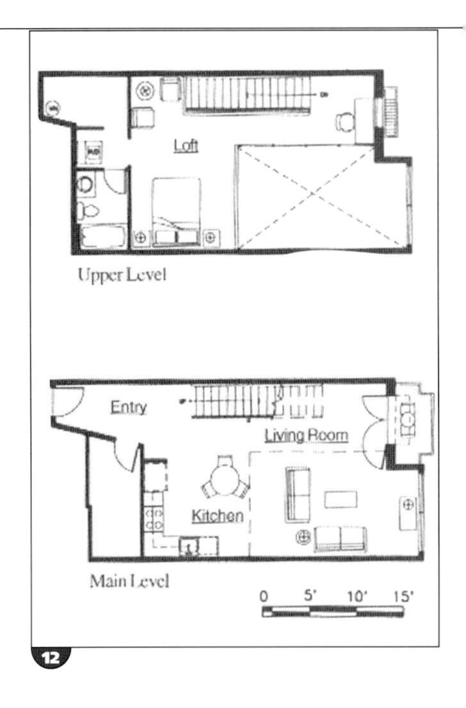

development costs

	Total	Cost per Dwelling Unit	Cost per Residential Square Foot
Site Acquisition Cost	$5,400,000	$12,100	$8.52
Site Improvement Cost	$12,000,000	$26,900	$18.92
Construction Cost	$45,800,000	$102,700	$72.23
Soft Costs	$13,100,000	$29,400	$20.66
Total Cost	$76,300,000	$171,100	$120.33

unit information

Unit Type	Lot Size (Square Feet)	Floor Area (Square Feet)	Number Planned/ Built	Current Sales Prices
Detached				
2-bdrm/2 1/2-bath	4,500	1,427	42/25	$194,000
2-bdrm/2-bath	4,500	1,447	43/26	$195,000
3-bdrm/2 1/2-bath	4,500	1,691	44/27	$207,000
3-bdrm/2 1/2-bath	4,500	1,706	45/28	$222,000
Townhouse				
2-bdrm/2-bath	3,500	1,208	27/17	$164,000
2-bdrm/2 1/2-bath	3,500	1,446	34/20	$178,000
2-bdrm/2 1/2-bath	3,500	1,669	27/17	$187,000
Loft Condominium				
Studio and 2-bdrm/2 bath	2,000	712–1,945	N/A	$129,900 and up

case study

crawford square

pittsburgh, pennsylvania

Crawford Square mends a great tear in Pittsburgh's urban fabric. The 426-unit project has taken a giant void in the city—18 acres of land cleared for urban renewal after the 1960s riots—and stitched it back into the fabric of the existing community. A blending of single-family and multifamily, rental and for-sale, and market-rate and subsidized housing, Crawford Square has been designed with a keen eye toward the architectural and social nuances of the Hill District, to which it is tied.

Located on the eastern edge of downtown Pittsburgh, the Hill District was once a thriving community known for its jazz clubs and ethnic diversity. Gravely wounded by the riots that followed the assassination of Dr. Martin Luther King, Jr., the neighborhood suffered further from the wholesale demolition of homes attendant to the construction of the nearby Civic Arena. With thousands of Lower Hill residents displaced by the arena and its parking lots, the community organized against further commercial encroachment, drawing the line at Crawford Street.

By the late 1980s, the Urban Redevelopment Authority (URA) of Pittsburgh had acquired much of the land for the first phase of Crawford Square and had issued a request for qualifications from developers. Based on its strong track record of successful inner-city redevelopment, the St. Louis–based development firm McCormack Baron Associates was selected as the developer for the project. McCormack Baron then enlisted the services of Pittsburgh-based Urban Design Associates (UDA), an architectural firm that also had

Note: Images for this case study are courtesy of Urban Design Associates.

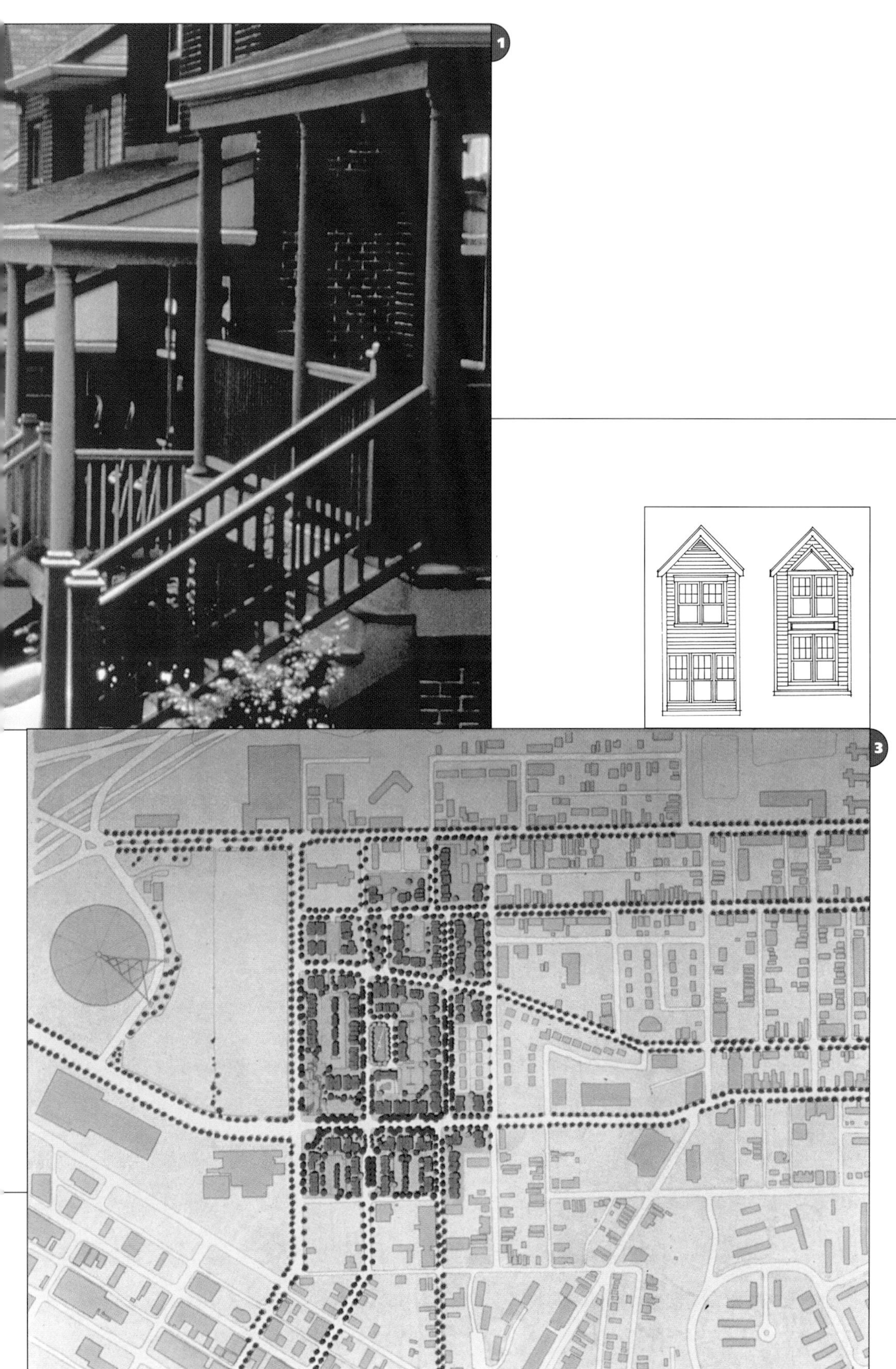

1, 2

In the shadow of downtown's office towers, Crawford Square returns a traditional urban neighborhood to the Hill District, replacing much that was lost to urban renewal efforts of the 1960s.

3

Site plan within its urban context.

4

strong credentials in inner-city redevelopment, to design the master plan for the project.

The master planning process was guided, and heavily influenced, by public participation. A project committee—consisting of local community leaders, residents, and the development team—was formed. After numerous meetings, a clear preference emerged: to develop a traditional Pittsburgh residential neighborhood, evoking the scale, density, and architectural style of the older East End neighborhoods. UDA conducted formal surveys to determine the characteristics that defined these neighborhoods and integrated these design principles into the master plan and design guidelines.

Demographically, the project committee sought to establish a mixed-income neighborhood, with a wide range of price points and housing types—apartments, townhouses, and single-family homes. The project committee was adamant, however, that Crawford Square should not have the look of a subsidized project and should be designed with the same high-quality standards and amenities of a fully market-rate development. As built, about half of the rental units in Crawford Square are subsidized, and they are indistinguishable from the market-rate units. In addition, the subsidized units periodically are rotated throughout the project, further blurring their identities.

The master plan created by UDA sought to restore the fine grain of the Hill District neighborhood. A grid of streets and blocks was designed, connecting to the adjacent streets. Each block, in turn, has its own character and scale, relating to the adjacent development. The narrowest streets, lined with single-family houses, are 30 feet in width, curb to curb. The wider streets, developed with townhouses and apartments, are 40 feet wide.

While the master plan sought to reestablish connections to the Hill District and the downtown core, at the same time the plan included measures to calm the traffic that flows through the neighborhood. The new Protectory Place, for example, has a wide, tree-lined median that splits and slows traffic as it passes through the community. Similarly, several intersections in the community are bulbed, to slow traffic, and stop signs are present at all intersections.

The master plan did not include retail or other commercial development, in deference to the existing nearby commercial areas. The injection of new residents into the neighborhood has, in fact, helped to attract a new supermarket to the Phoenix Hill Shopping Center, adjacent to Crawford Square.

Applying new urbanist principles to its inner-city site, UDA's design guidelines for Crawford Square set new housing close to the street and encouraged front porches. Building setbacks are typically 20 to 25 feet from the property line with porches set forward of the setback. The steep 15 percent slope of the site precluded the development of alleys and rear-loaded garages that might be expected in a traditionally designed neighborhood, but the front-loaded garages are typically set 12 feet lower than the raised front porches, visually minimizing the garages. Apartment buildings and townhouses form a perimeter around the parking areas, hiding them from view. An electronic key card is required to enter these parking areas.

4

Within the urban grid, neighborhood parks provide open space for residents.

5

A block of apartments maintains the character and scale of the single-family sections of the neighborhood. Streets are bulbed to calm traffic without closing off vehicular access.

6, 7

Single-family houses are similar in style and form to those built in the East End neighborhoods in the early part of the 20th century. Because of Pittsburgh's hilly terrain, garages commonly occupy the lower level and are reached from a sloped driveway at the front of the house.

The master plan called for housing in the colonial revival motif, common in East End neighborhoods. The homes feature tall, narrow windows, bay windows, dormers, and gable ends facing the street. To evoke a sense of quality and stability, facades are constructed of brick and clapboard siding. All buildings—single-family, multifamily, and apartments—are two to three stories in height, with front yards and backyards. Apartment buildings and townhouses have rear courtyards. To avoid a "cookie-cutter" appearance, building types are varied within the same block, townhouses are set in groups of no more than five units, and the front plane of each townhouse is varied relative to its neighbors. Also, to encourage variation in design, different architectural firms were hired to design the buildings for Phase II and Phase III.

Amenities at Crawford Square include a community center and swimming pool for the residents' use. To further connect Crawford Square with the wider community, the land plan established three new public parks.

Resident safety was a key concern in the design of Crawford Square. Setting front porches and houses close to the street was intended not only to encourage interaction among residents but also to put "eyes on the street." Similarly, the low decorative light posts serve to keep the neighborhood well lit. Overall, the intention of the master plan was to leave no "unclaimed" space. As a further deterrent to crime, a few city police officers were offered reduced rents to encourage them to relocate to the neighborhood. Despite some initial concerns, crime has been practically nonexistent.

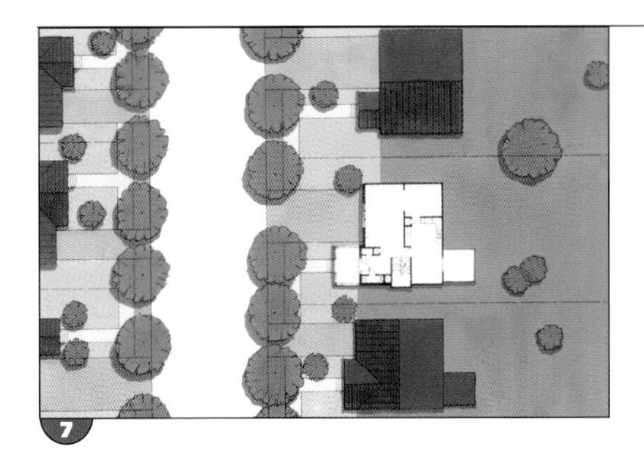

8

Typical townhouse plan.

9

Townhouses are modeled after traditional East End duplexes with mirror image facades.

10

Design guidelines were established for Crawford Square similar to those in the house pattern books of the early 20th century. They set rules to ensure consistent quality and character for the community despite numerous builders, price points, and development phases. Rather than present specific house plans, the guidelines establish standards for setbacks, scale, materials, and such key architectural elements as windows, porches, and doors. It is up to the individual builder to put it all together.

Phase I of Crawford Square, completed in 1993, consists of 203 rental apartments and townhomes, with 50 percent of the units subsidized. In the second and third phases of the development, the rental program was scaled back in favor of more for-sale housing, based on resident preferences and market pressure. In Phase II, completed in 1995, 71 new rental units and 30 for-sale units were developed. In Phase III, to be completed in 2000, 74 rental units and 21 additional for-sale units are being developed.

In response to the scale-back of the rental program, McCormack Baron partnered with the Hill Community Development Corporation (HCDC) in the second and third phases of the development. McCormack Baron continued to develop and manage the rental units, while the HCDC assumed responsibility for development of for-sale housing.

Conventional financing was inadequate for Crawford Square. The financing package, particularly for Phase I, was complex and multilayered. In addition to the equity contributed by the developer and obtained through the sale of low-income housing tax credits, four other financing sources were used. These included the Urban

9

Redevelopment Authority of Pittsburgh (loans and grants); the Pennsylvania Housing Finance Agency (loans and bond proceeds); a consortium of four local lenders: PNC Bank, Mellon Bank, Dollar Bank, and Integra Bank (loans and grants); and a consortium of local foundations (grants). "Each participant was necessary to the deal and provided an element of credibility that convinced the others to be involved," says Vince Bennett, vice president of McCormack Baron. "The withdrawal of support [by] any partner could have stopped the development. Spreading the financial risk both increased the community's sense of responsibility and ensured that the project would be done without sacrificing the quality or scope, and that it would be affordable to a diverse population."

Of concern in any mixed-income development is the ability to attract market-rate residents. To the surprise and delight of the development team, market-rate units in Crawford Square have leased-up faster than subsidized units, and for-sale housing demand has been exceptionally strong as well. Pent-up demand for high-quality in-town housing and Crawford Square's exceptional location and downtown views have worked to attract a mix of residents, both economically and racially. Rents range from about $300 per month for some one-bedroom apartments to $1,200 per month for a three-bedroom townhouse. For-sale housing starts at about $89,000, and some four-bedroom units in the final phase of the development are selling for as much as $200,000. About 80 percent of residents are African American, many of them former Hill District residents brought back to their old neighborhood by the availability of new, high-quality housing.

Special financing incentives were provided to homebuyers in the first phase of development. These included a $15,000 grant from the U.S. Department of Housing and Urban Development and a mortgage subsidy of $25,000 from the Urban Redevelopment Authority of Pittsburgh. In light of the unexpectedly strong demand, however, these offers were significantly scaled back in later phases.

"What Crawford Square has leveraged is as important as what it is," according to Barry Long, UDA's project manager. As "one of the first successful inner-city examples of new urbanism," he adds, "the community serves as a model for future redevelopment activities." Building on the success of Crawford Square, representatives of the neighborhood and city officials now are planning for the extension of new infill development to the remainder of the Hill District.

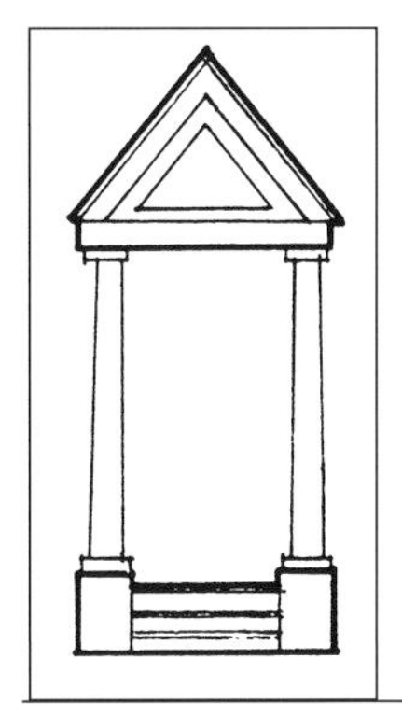

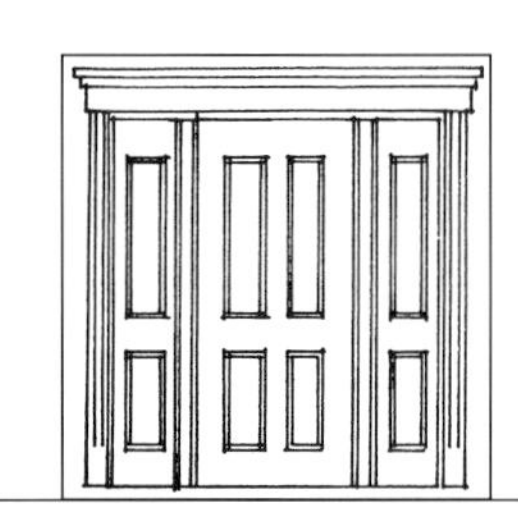

case study

crawford square

pittsburgh, pennsylvania

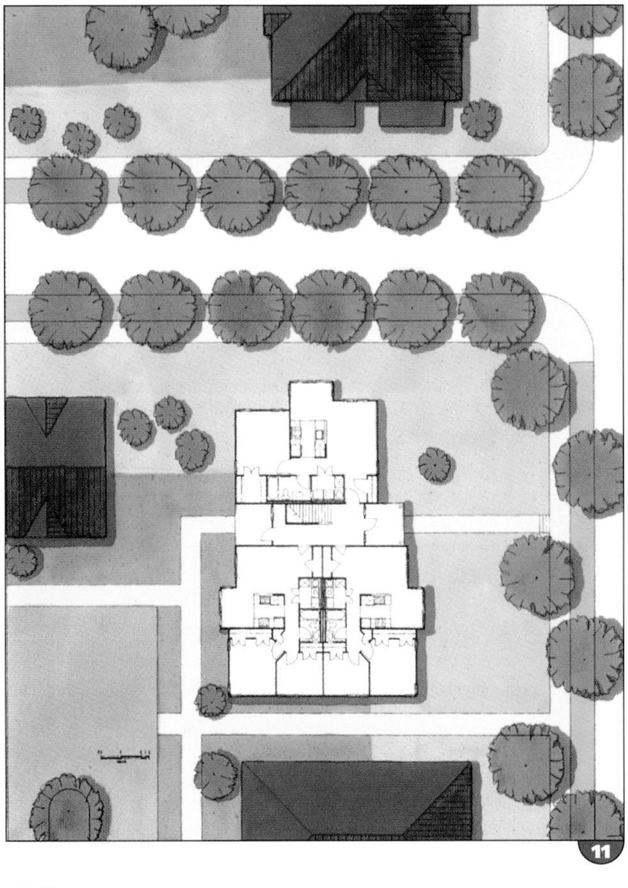

land use information

Site Area:	24.0 acres	
Total Dwelling Units:	426, in three phases	
Gross Project Density:	17.8 units per acre	
Gross Residential Density:	18.4 units per acre	
Housing Types:	Rental and for-sale apartments, townhomes, and single-family homes	
Parking Total:	304 spaces	
Parking Ratio:	0.71 spaces/unit	
Project Completion Dates:	Phase I	1993
	Phase II	1995
	Phase III	2000

land use plan

	Acres	Percent of Site
Residential	15.2	63.3%
Recreation/Amenities	0.8	3.4%
Roads/Parking[1]	8.0	33.3%
Total	24.0	100.0%

[1]Includes public streets within project.

11, 12

Low-rise apartments echo the scale of the original Hill District neighborhood before urban renewal clearance.

contact information

Developer	McCormack Baron Associates Hadley Square 1101 Lucas Avenue St. Louis, Missouri 63101 314-621-3400
Master Planner	Urban Design Associates Gulf Tower, 31st Floor 707 Grant Street Pittsburgh, Pennsylvania 15219 412-263-5200
Landscape Architect	La Quatra Bonci 95 South Tenth Street Pittsburgh, Pennsylvania 15203 412-488-8822
Phase II Architect	Tai & Lee Architects 3114 Bereton Street Pittsburgh, Pennsylvania 15219 412-681-8832
Phase III Architect (Rental)	Trivers Associates 100 North Broadway, Suite 1800 St. Louis, Missouri 63102 314-241-2900

development costs

Rental Housing	Total	Cost per Dwelling Unit	Cost per Residential Square Foot
Phase I	$18,667,000	$91,955	$109.28
Phase II	$8,000,000	$112,676	$128.89
Phase III	$7,285,000	$98,445	N/A
Total	$33,952,000		
For-Sale Housing			
Phase I	$3,469,871	$128,481	
Phase II	$4,981,025	$166,034	
Total	$8,450,896		

unit information

Unit Type	Number	Size Range (Square Feet)	Price/Rent	
Phase I (Rental)			**Market**	**Affordable**
Garden: 1-bdrm/1-bath	61	675–703	$560	$364
Garden: 2-bdrm/1-bath	80	862	$640	$437
Split Townhouse: 1-bdrm/1-bath	21	696–698	$600	$364
Split Townhouse: 2-bdrm/2-bath	21	1,154–1,009	$775	$437
Townhouse: 2-bdrm/1 1/2-bath	12	1,006	$750	$437
Townhouse: 3-bdrm/1 1/2-bath	8	1,205	$875	$488
(For-Sale)				
Townhouses	9	1,200–1,450	$89,500–$138,900	
Detached	18	1,210–1,820	N/A	
Phase II (Rental)				
Garden: 1-bdrm	19	674 average	N/A	
Garden: 2-bdrm	27	880 average	N/A	
Townhouse: 2-bdrm	15	880 average	N/A	
Townhouse: 3-bdrm	10	1,230 average	N/A	
(For-Sale)				
Townhouse	7	N/A	$93,900–$141,000	
Detached	23	N/A	N/A	
Phase III	74	N/A	N/A	

case study

The Pointe at Lincoln Park

Chicago, Illinois

The Pointe is a 154-unit townhouse project set amid the 19th-century rowhouses of Chicago's Lincoln Park neighborhood. Occupying the site of a former hospital, the limestone and brick townhouses follow the triangular street grid bordering the site, resulting in a series of small—and very private—interior courtyards. Along Lincoln Avenue, the neighborhood's primary thoroughfare, the townhouses are four stories in height. They are composed of stacked units, each two stories high. Along the quieter side streets, the townhouses are three stories in height and doubled front to back, providing both street-fronting units and courtyard-fronting units.

The first developer that tried to redevelop the seven-acre site proposed a 19-story tower, which quickly encountered neighborhood opposition. A second proposal—for an eight-story building—also was opposed by the community. In response to these failed proposals, the MCL Companies proposed a low-rise alternative: a contextual project that met the neighborhood's concern for continuity with the past as well as the developer's need for a project of sufficient density to be financially feasible.

Taking a cue from the historic neighborhood, the Pointe's townhouses were sited close to the street. The units are set back 11 feet from the front property line, which, in turn, is eight to 12 feet back from the curb. True to the vernacular, the small front yards are set off from the sidewalk by iron gates. Unit entries are paired and raised on stone stoops.

The Pointe's site plan has a strong formal logic. One enters the project along Lincoln Avenue through a symmetrical pair of "gateway" buildings. These structures—the "gateway to the Lincoln Avenue Renaissance," as they have been dubbed—are actually fourplex townhouses crowned by conical copper roofs.

Limestone portals, at midblock along Lincoln Avenue, break up the long expanse of townhouses and provide pedestrian access to the interior open spaces and townhouses of the project. These arched and columned pedestrianways, set perpendicular to Lincoln Avenue, are formal and ceremonial in feeling and also

1

Adrienne Schmitz

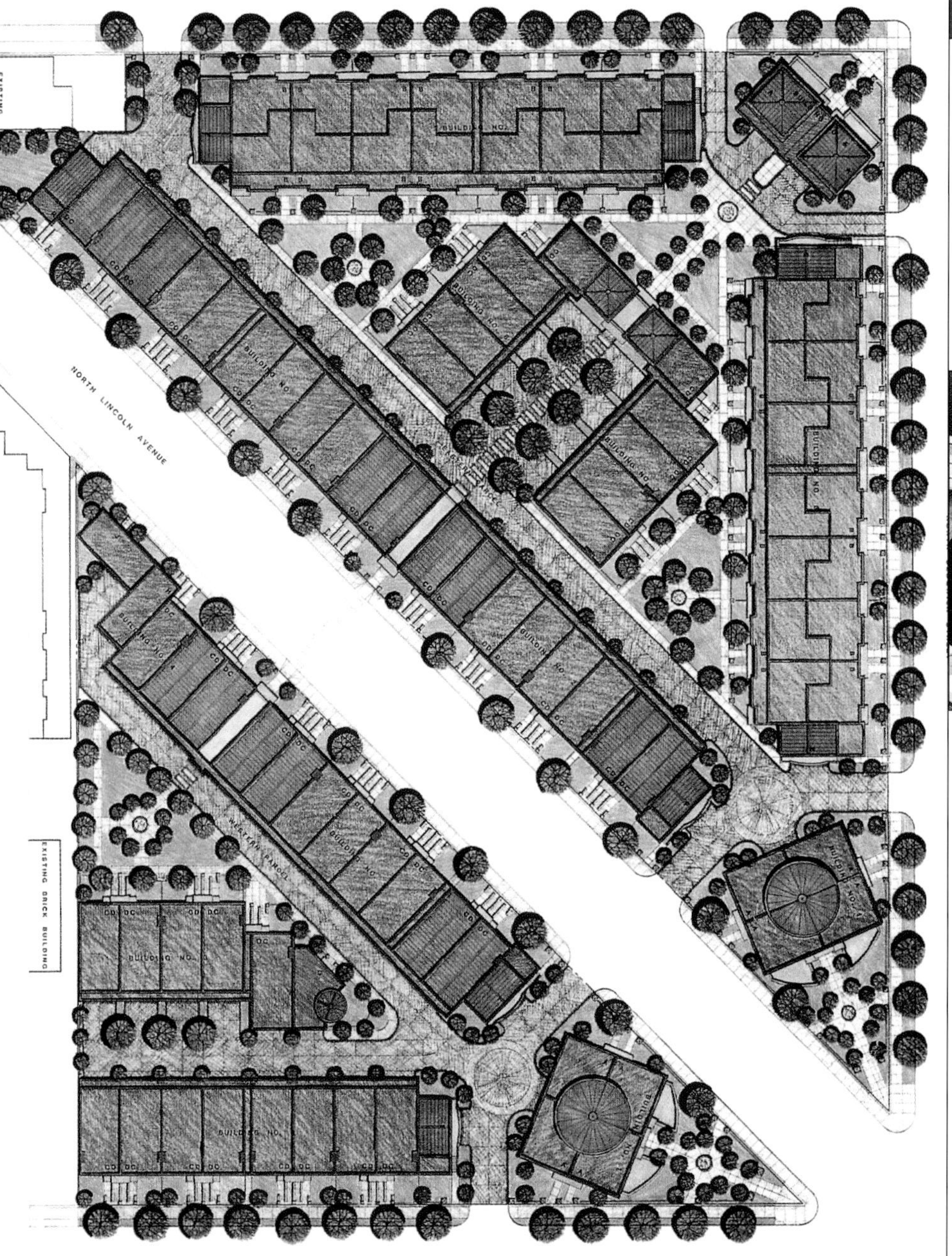

1, 2

The Pointe at Lincoln Park, a luxury development of stacked two-level units, opens its doors directly onto the urban streetscape. Front stoops, iron fencing, and formal limestone and brick elevations recall Chicago's traditional architecture, in contemporary form.

3

The formal plan incorporates pedestrian walkways and private landscaped spaces.

MCL Companies/Michael Kardas

notably open. Although there are no gates or bars on the portals, these narrow passages are in effect self-policing: "Anyone not living there is clearly out of place," notes MCL's president, Dan McLean. The passages are carefully monitored by residents.

For the "over-and-under" stacked units, parking is provided at grade level, accessed from a rear driveway. Each unit has a single-car garage and an apron parking space. Residents in the "under" units go directly from the parking garage into their dwelling units. Residents of the "over" units walk up to their living spaces on the third and fourth floors.

The back-to-back units have two-car "garages" within a communal parking structure. The communal parking is located at grade—beneath the living quarters—and entered from either end of the townhouse row. In lieu of open stalls, however, as in a standard parking structure, residents can close a residential-type garage door behind them, effectively incorporating the two parking stalls into the residence.

Roy H. Kruse & Associates/Robert J. Heidrich

4

Eliminating exterior driveways for the back-to-back units allows these units to have front doors that open directly onto the interior courtyards. Enclosed by building walls, the courtyards have the feeling of urban squares, complete with tiled walkways and manicured lawns, coach lights, and formally planted flowerbeds.

The first floor of the townhouses is clad in alternating bands of rusticated limestone and "Renaissance stone" blocks fabricated to simulate limestone. Windows and cornices also are trimmed in the white limestone, contrasting with the red brick facades and deep green of the tall, multipane windows. The top floor of the townhouses is set back from the face of the building to provide additional private outdoor space for residents. This rooftop deck area, which doubles as a required exitway for the four-story units, is partially hidden behind high parapet walls.

In the interior, living rooms, dining rooms, and kitchens typically have oak floors and nine- or ten-foot ceilings. Bedrooms and family rooms, located on the upper floors, have eight-foot ceilings and are carpeted. "Architecture definitely counts in the city of Chicago," notes Tamara Laber, vice president of sales and marketing for MCL, in reference to the extensive use of limestone detailing and other expensive design features.

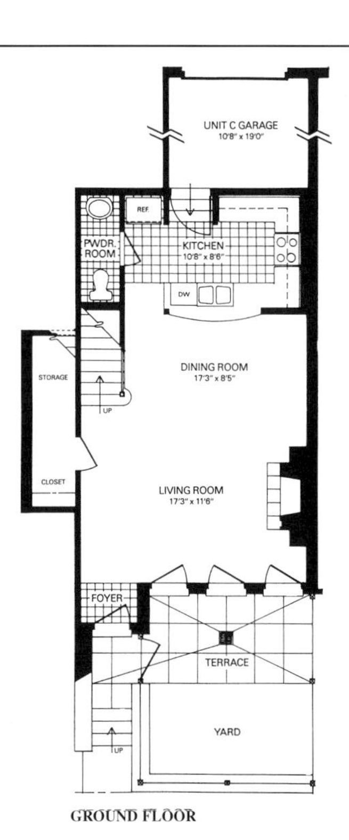

GROUND FLOOR

SECOND FLOOR

5

4

Parking courts with garages are located at the rear in order not to interfere with the more formal pedestrian spaces.

5

Typical two-bedroom unit.

6

The formality of the street face is carried into landscaped interior courtyards. Units have entrances facing either the street or courtyards.

Roy H. Kruse & Associates/Robert J. Heidrich

The Pointe's 154 townhouses sold out in six months, an average absorption rate of 26 units per month. Masked by the average absorption statistic is an even more startling statistic: signed contracts were taken for all 96 units in the first phase (the parcel north of Lincoln Avenue) in just one week. The very rapid absorption was due in part, notes MCL's Dan McLean, to the wide range of unit types and prices ($279,000 to $509,000) offered at the Pointe.

The lowest-priced units, which are the lower units of the stacked Lincoln Avenue townhouses, appealed to first-time homebuyers, singles, and professional couples. Some of these buyers were trading up from condominiums. Many came from within a mile and a half of the site. The upper units, priced at $419,000, and the larger (approximately 3,000-square-foot) units along the side streets appealed to move-up buyers, some of whom were families with children. Other higher-priced units were

Roy H. Kruse & Associates/Robert J. Heidrich

7

The "gateway buildings," which flank the Lincoln Avenue spine of the project, face the main streets with rounded towers capped with conical copper roofs.

8

Typical three-bedroom unit.

sold to empty nesters, including some returning to city living after raising children in the suburbs. The back-to-back units had a similarly wide appeal; as many buyers preferred the courtyard units as the street-facing units, notes Dan McLean.

"There's a huge back-to-the-city movement in Chicago," says McLean. "Ten years ago, perhaps 20 percent of buyers were 'move backs.' Today, that number approaches 40 to 50 percent in some projects," he notes. Unit sizes are getting larger, as well. "Ten years ago," McLean continues, "developers offered a smaller product to a somewhat pioneering young buyer." Now, developers like MCL are offering units as large as those of their suburban counterparts to buyers who have the means to choose either type of location. At MCL's Central Station project, just south of the downtown Loop, MCL has been selling 3,000- to 3,800-square-foot townhouses in the range of $500,000 to $700,000. The common denominator, notes McLean, is that cities have attractions that the suburbs do not have—and, given the opportunity, many homebuyers prefer city living.

8

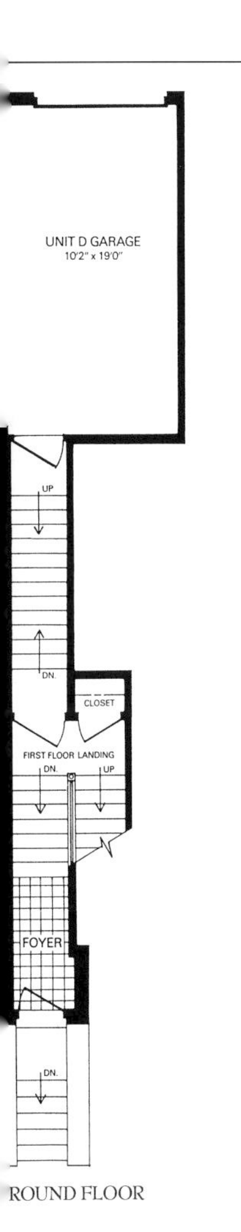

ROUND FLOOR

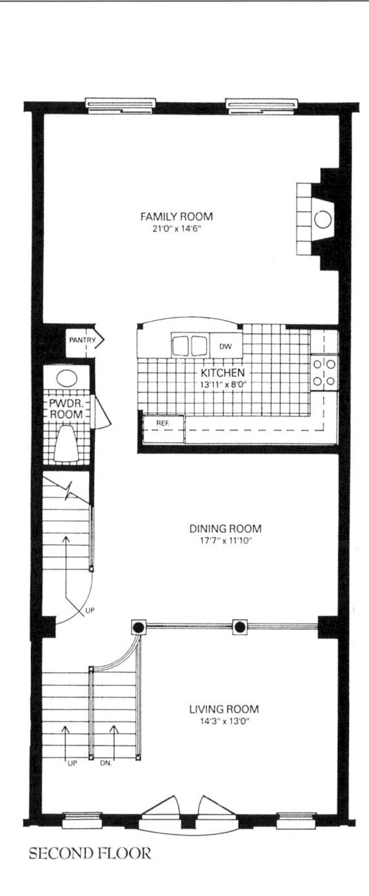

SECOND FLOOR

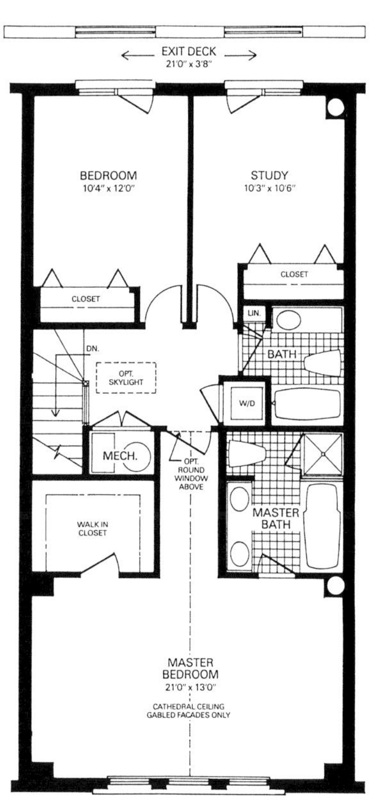

THIRD FLOOR

case study

The Pointe at Lincoln Park

Chicago, Illinois

land use information

Site Area:	7.0 acres
Total Dwelling Units:	154
Gross Project Density:	22 units per acre
Housing Type:	Townhouses (7 designs)
Gross Residential Density:	23.6 units per acre
Parking Total:	208 spaces
Parking Ratio:	1.3 spaces/unit
Project Completion Date:	June 1997

land use plan

	Acres	Percentage of Site
Residential	5.70	81.4%
Roads/Parking	0.75	10.7%
Open Space	0.55	7.9%
Total	7.00	100.0%

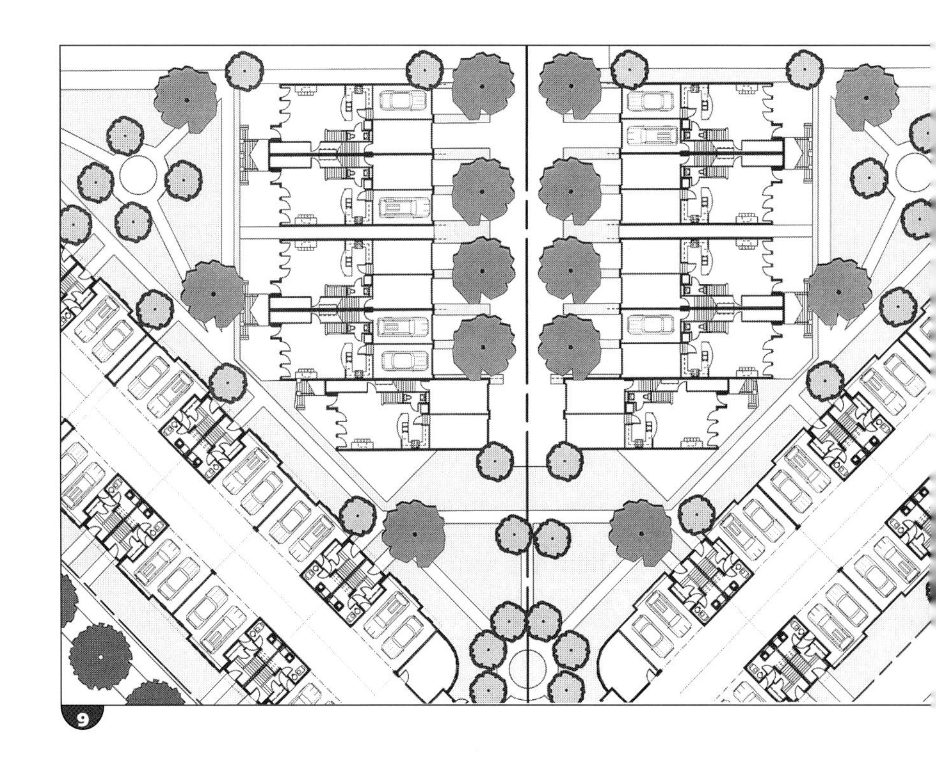

9

Ground-floor plan shows back-to-back units (diagonal buildings) with communal garage under units. Interior buildings have individual garages, reached from the rear parking courts.

10

The courtyards can be reached directly from Lincoln Avenue by way of pedestrian portals that indicate the privacy of the space without the use of secured gates.

development costs

	Total	Cost per Dwelling Unit	Cost per Residential Square Foot
Site Acquisition Cost	$13,560,000	$89,211	$42.17
Site Improvement Cost	$2,900,000	$19,079	$9.02
Construction Cost	$33,700,000	$221,711	$104.80
Soft Costs	$9,300,000	$61,184	$28.92
Total Development Cost	$59,460,000	$391,185	$184.91

unit information

Unit Type	Floor Area (Square Feet)	Number	Final Sales Prices
2-bdrm/2 1/2-bath	1,721	52	$279,900
2-bdrm/2 1/2-bath	2,505	52	$419,900
3-bdrm/3 1/2-bath	3,117	32	$499,900
3-bdrm/2 1/2 -bath	2,825	8	$509,900
Various	2,558–3,566	10	N/A
Total		154	

contact information

Developer	MCL Companies 455 East Illinois Street Suite 565 Chicago, Illinois 60611 312-321-8900
Architect	Roy H. Kruse & Associates 833 West Chicago Avenue Suite 200 Chicago, Illinois 60618 312-563-1102
Landscape	Landscape by Design P.O. Box 115 Winnetka, Illinois 60093 800-498-5296

case study

Metro Senior Housing & Citypark

Foster City, California

In the 1960s, when the suburban San Francisco town of Foster City was master planned, a site was set aside for a town center, complete with village green. Twenty years later, by the early 1980s, the community and its town center were essentially built out, with the highly noticeable exception of the village green and two small parcels flanking the green to the east and west. A high-rise office tower had been built on the north side of the green and a retail center on the south side. The green itself was at that point little more than a mound of unkempt grass and debris, avoided by office workers and shoppers alike.

Today, the town center is complete, neatly stitched together by a redesigned town green and 102 units of housing. The housing is mixed both in type—low-rise townhouses and mid-rise apartments—and in tenure—market-rate for-sale housing, and assisted rental housing for seniors. And, in a bold and somewhat unusual move, the two housing types were integrated within each of the residential parcels. "The first thought," notes Alexander Seidel, principal of Seidel/Holzman Architects, was, "you'll take one side and I'll take the other," referring to the usual turf wars between for-sale housing and assisted rental housing. But given the site's symmetry and the city's interest in integrating the housing types, a hybrid was designed that deftly combines the two types of housing into mutually supportive urban "villages."

The focus of the project—and the key to making the housing density work—is the acre-and-a-half town green. Designed as a circle within a square, and paved with two-tone bands of brick, the green has a wide ceremonial north-south axis, linking the office and retail uses. It also has a more intimate east-west pathway, drawing in the housing on either side of the green. At the center is a small plaza with a clock tower, a favored meeting place for office workers, residents, and the town at large.

The green has an urban feeling, with its continuous townhouse facades on either side, and an urbane layering of landscape and circulation elements that psychologically separates the public park from the semipublic townhouse walkways and the private town-

©Seidel/Holzman, photo by Tom Rider

1

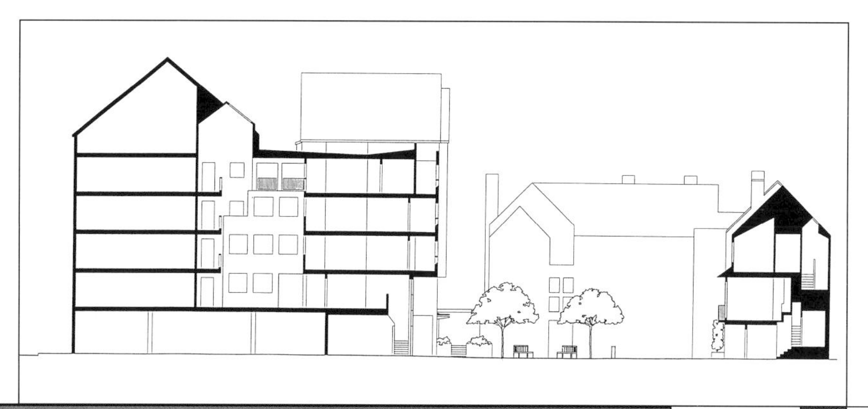

1, 2

The project combines for-sale townhouses and subsidized rental apartments for seniors and is anchored by a public square. The landscaped square has become a popular gathering spot for residents, nearby workers, and shoppers.

3

Building cross section shows relationship between townhouses and apartments, with landscaped and paved areas as the focal point.

©Seidel/Holzman, photo by Tom Rider

4, 5

Through careful massing of form and color, the five-story apartment buildings maintain the character and scale of the townhouses. Steep metal roofs also help to give the larger buildings a more residential scale.

6

The symmetric plan incorporates a town square, market-rate townhouses and subsidized seniors' housing in a configuration in which each element enhances the others. Twin residential villages are located at opposite ends of the square; each includes townhouses wrapped around apartment buildings. Vehicular access is shared by the townhouses and apartments, with garages located off paved courts.

house entries. The green's great circle is edged with a continuous concrete bench, which defines the outer edge of the public realm. Beyond the concrete ring, hedges and trees provide a further visual separation between the park and the townhouses. The townhouses themselves are raised up a half flight with old-fashioned stoops to provide an added layer of privacy to what is a very public context.

The three-story townhouses are arranged in U-shaped patterns held close to the adjacent streets as well as to the town green. The townhouses wrap around and enclose the five-story buildings for seniors, as well as the parking courts that run between them. The parking courts, which are paved with interlocking asphalt pavers, serve as secondary streets, providing access to the townhouses and seniors' parking, and to a dropoff at the front door of each seniors' building. The townhouses have two-car garages (arranged in tandem fashion) tucked under the two-story living quarters. Seniors park in the single-level at-grade garage within each seniors' building.

Steven Fader

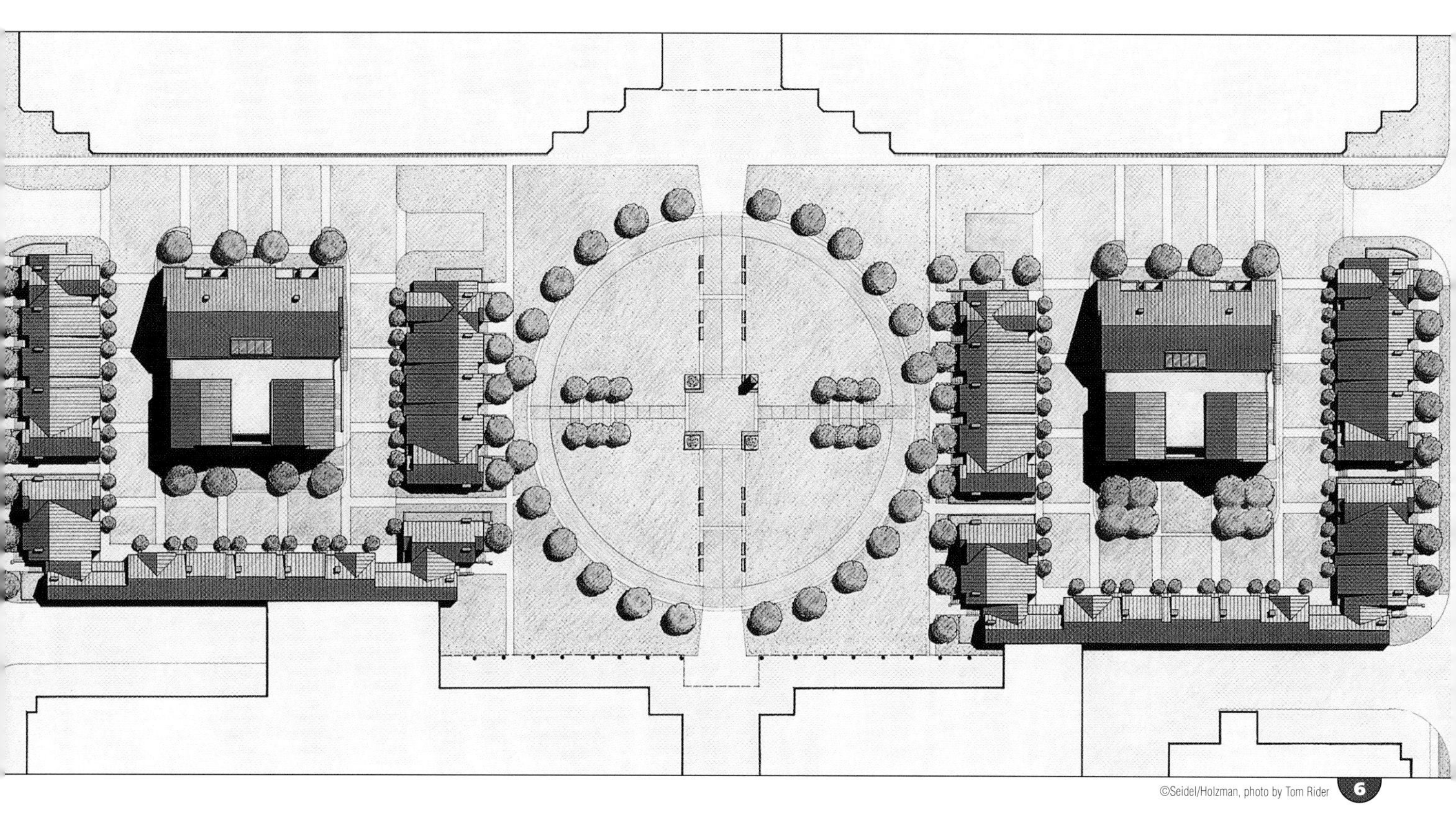

©Seidel/Holzman, photo by Tom Rider 6

Below-grade parking, which might have been preferable, was precluded because of the high water table at the site.

The design of the project is modern in sensibility and yet clearly anchored to a more traditional residential idiom, with its pitched rooflines, stoops, and bays. Roofs are constructed of metal, which was a city requirement for the project, and one that further bridges the gap between the traditional and the contemporary. Exterior walls are gray and yellow stucco, accenting the varied massing of the structures.

The townhouses are arranged in groups of six or seven units, designed to be read both individually and as an ensemble. At the unit level, there is a clear rhythm of bay windows, stoops, and metal-topped chimneys. As a grouping, the multiunit buildings are balanced compositionally, with gabled units on each end, tied together by a horizontal molding course.

For seniors, the project design provides a variety of indoor and outdoor spaces in which to congregate and makes it possible to satisfy most daily needs without a car. Each seniors' building is organized around a four-story central atrium that opens onto a small landscaped exterior sitting area. Breezeways cut through the enclosing townhouses and link the seniors' housing to the town green, which in turn provides access to the adjacent shopping center.

The greatest challenge of inserting the two housing blocks into the existing urban pattern was dealing with the loading and access requirements of the adjacent office building and retail center. Partial redesign of these facilities was required in order to insulate the residential uses from the noise and activity of these adjacencies. The rules regarding permissible hours for deliveries and activities were also tightened.

Development of Metro Senior Housing & CityPark resulted from an intense public/private partnership. The evolving design

©Seidel/Holzman, photo by Tom Rider

concepts were reviewed in numerous public study sessions that were attended by local residents and other stakeholders, including the merchants in the adjacent retail center. The sessions provided many insights, according to architect Alexander Seidel, which led to modifications and refinements to the plan. Overseeing the entire project was the Foster City Redevelopment Agency. Regis Homes was the developer of the market-rate component of the project and the builder for the entire project. BRIDGE Housing Corporation, one of the most active builders of subsidized housing in northern California, was brought in by Regis as developer of the seniors' housing.

Financing for the project came from a variety of sources: the city used its "in-lieu" fees collected from developers of other citywide projects to finance the town green improvements. Tax increment bond financing and housing tax credits were employed for the seniors' housing, and conventional construction financing was obtained for the townhouse component. The latter was a hard sell, because of the unorthodox mixing of market-rate and assisted dwelling units, but financing was ultimately obtained at standard rates and terms.

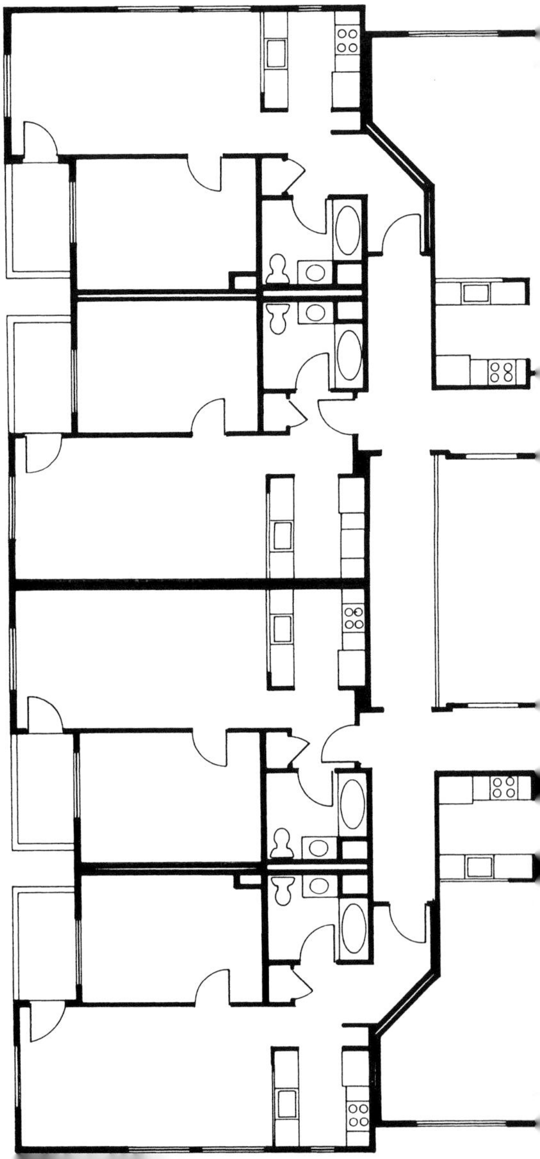

7

A four-story atrium sitting area forms the core of each of the seniors' buildings. In addition, each building has a private outdoor space.

8

A symbiotic relationship exists between the residences and the town square. The buildings enclose the square and give it intimacy, while the square provides attractive open space for the residences.

9

Metro Senior Housing: first floor plan.

Steven Fader

8

9

The 42 CityPark townhouses sold for $270,000 to $300,000 in 1996. Originally there was some concern about marketing relatively high-end townhouses located so close to low-income renters, but this proved not to be a problem. The townhouses sold out in seven months, an average of six units per month. There was "no discernible loss of value in the market-rate housing from being close to the assisted housing," notes Alexander Seidel. In fact, just the opposite occurred: resale prices for the townhouses spiked 30 percent in the first year.

Metro Senior Housing & CityPark has been successful by other measures as well. The town green, once a space to avoid, is now frequented by office workers and city residents. Outdoor concerts share the green with everyday strollers. Retail sales in the adjacent shopping center reportedly have increased. "There is an anxiety about density," notes Alexander Seidel, but the issue is not whether density is good or bad. Rather, says Seidel, we should be speaking in terms of "good or bad solutions to density." Clearly, the right solution has been found in Foster City.

case study

Metro Senior Housing & CityPark

Foster City, California

land use information

Site Area:	3.64 acres
Total Dwelling Units:	102
Gross Project Density:	28.0 units per acre
Housing Types:	Townhouses and apartments
Average Lot Size:	902 square feet
Gross Residential Density:	44.3 units per acre
Parking, Total:	134 spaces
Parking Ratio:	1.3 spaces/unit
Project Completion Date:	December 1996

land use plan

	Acres	Percentage of Site
Residential	1.24	34%
Roads/Parking	1.06	29%
Open Space	1.34	37%
Total	3.64	100%

contact information

Developer (Townhouses)	Regis Homes 393 Vintage Park Drive, #100 Foster City, California 94404 650-377-5702
Developer (Seniors' Housing)	BRIDGE Housing Corporation One Hawthorne Street, 4th floor San Francisco, California 94105 415-989-1111
Architect	Seidel/Holzman 425 Battery Street, 3rd floor San Francisco, California 94111 415-397-5535
Architect of Record (Townhouses)	James Guthrie Associates One Waters Park Drive, #108 San Mateo, California 94403
Landscape Architect	Guzardo & Associates 836 Montgomery Street San Francisco, California 94111 415-433-4672
Public Agency	Foster City Redevelopment Agency 610 Foster City Boulevard Foster City, California 94404 650-349-1200

10

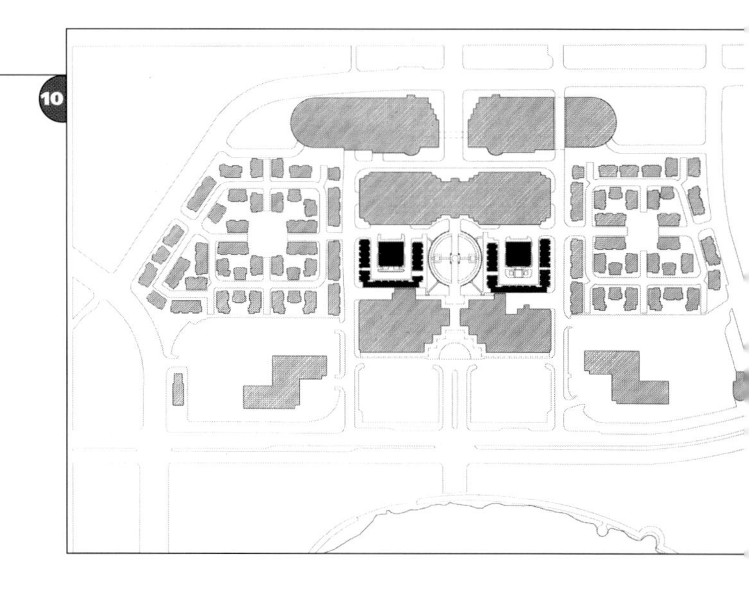

development costs: townhouses and town green

	Total	Cost per Dwelling Unit	Cost per Residential Square Foot
Site Acquisition Cost	$840,000	$20,000	$13.80
Site Improvement Cost	$1,050,000	$25,000	$17.20
Construction Cost	$4,993,000	$119,000	$82.00
Soft Costs	$2,183,000	$52,000	$36.00
Total Development Cost	$9,066,000	$216,000	$149.00

unit information

Unit Type	Floor Area (Square Feet)	Number	Final Sales Prices
3-bdrm/2 1/2-bath	1,550	28	$290,000
3-bdrm/2 1/2-bath	1,500	4	$280,000
2-bdrm/2 1/2-bath	1,150	10	$260,000
Total		42	

development costs: seniors' housing

	Total	Cost per Dwelling Unit	Cost per Residential Square Foot
Site Acquisition Cost	$800,000	$13,333	$17.98
Site Improvement Cost	$600,000	$10,000	$13.48
Construction Cost	$4,500,000	$75,000	$101.12
Soft Costs	$1,800,000	$30,000	$40.45
Total Development Cost	$7,700,000	$128,000	$173.03

unit information

Unit Type	Floor Area (Square Feet)	Number	Final Sales Prices or Rent
1-bdrm	670	48	Variable, based on income
2-bdrm	890	12	Variable, based on income
Total		60	

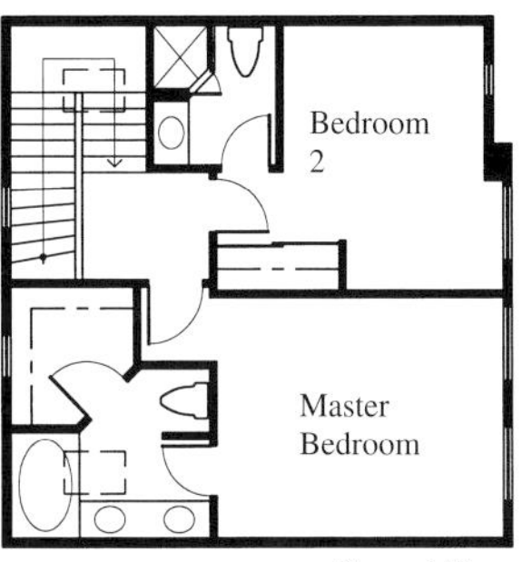

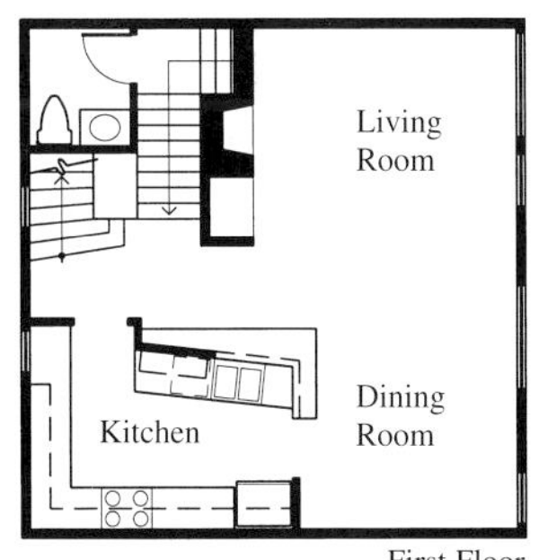

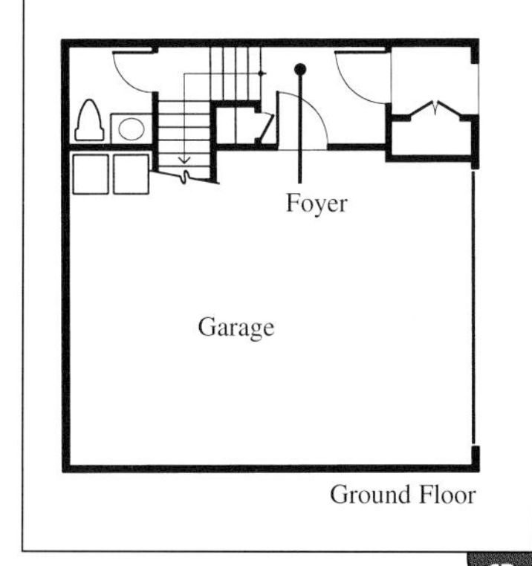

10

The project within its urban context.

11

Contemporary architectural styling makes use of traditional forms.

12

CityPark two-bedroom townhouse floor plan.

case study

Addison Circle

Addison, Texas

Addison Circle has brought density—and a sense of community—to a classic edge city. Located in Addison, Texas, a northern suburb of Dallas, the 80-acre mixed-use project is the result of a public/private partnership between Post Properties, Inc., and the town of Addison. Designed by RTKL Associates in conjunction with Post Properties and a team of consultants, Addison Circle ultimately will tally some 3,000 dwelling units intermixed with neighborhood retail, parks, and civic space, as well as up to 4 million square feet of offices and commercial uses. At about 55 dwelling units per acre (net), the mostly rental project is more than twice as dense as the typical north Dallas garden apartment project. Yet, Addison Circle has a sense of place and community not often seen in new development.

The idea for a higher-density, mixed-use, residential neighborhood was first suggested in Addison's 1991 comprehensive plan and more recently in a community-based "visioning" program (Vision 2020). The town of Addison always has attracted more than its share of commercial development. But as competition emerged from newer suburbs, Addison town officials focused on the need to create a physical focal point for the town—as well as a stronger population base—to support and anchor the town's commercial uses.

Although land-locked and about 80 percent built out, one of the few remaining undeveloped sites in Addison proved to be ideally suited to the concept of a higher-density, mixed-used development. The site, adjacent to Addison's Old Town, was within walking distance to

1

Note: Images for this case study courtesy of RTKL/Craig Blackmon.

employment, retail, and entertainment; it was adjacent to a Dallas Area Rapid Transit Station (DART), close to Addison's conference and theater center and, not incidentally, controlled by a single landowner. Encouraged by town officials, the landowner, Gaylord Properties, teamed with Post Properties, an Atlanta-based REIT to develop a program and plan for the site.

1

Addison Circle's plan is a pedestrian-friendly grid of streets and narrow mews, with the circle as a focal point. The community will ultimately include 3,000 dwelling units, neighborhood retail, and up to 4 million square feet of office and commercial space.

2, 3

Addison Circle brings dense urban forms to a suburban edge city. Residential neighborhoods consist of four-story buildings, some with retail businesses on the first floor.

As designed, the master plan for Addison Circle establishes two subareas: a residential neighborhood of mid-rise housing, with supporting retail uses, parks, and other amenities, and a higher-density office and commercial district adjacent to the North Dallas Tollway. Linking the two areas is an armature of open space: a traffic roundabout (Addison Circle) and an axial green.

Attention to streets and open space—public space in general—is one of the things that makes Addison Circle so appealing. The circle itself is the symbolic center of the project. But in addition to its symbolic role, the roundabout serves to calm traffic that flows along Quorum Drive, a preexisting major thoroughfare that cuts through the middle of the site. The roundabout did not come into being without controversy; a special roundabout consultant was required to convince skeptical officials to permit construction of what was to be the first public traffic circle in the area in more than 50 years. A design competition also was held to create a sculpture for the center of the circle, in order to further establish the circle as the focal point of the project and of the larger community.

Substantial investment is evident in the treatment of Addison Circle's residential streets and boulevards. Sidewalks and crosswalks in many

4

Buildings exude a solid permanence. Built of red brick with a course of stone at the base, they are finely detailed with painted metal balconies and cast stone arches and lintels.

5

Aerial view.

6

Buildings fronting the more major streets include neighborhood-serving retail on the first level. Mature trees line the sidewalks, providing shade for pedestrians. They also give the impression of a stable, well-established town, rather than a new development.

4

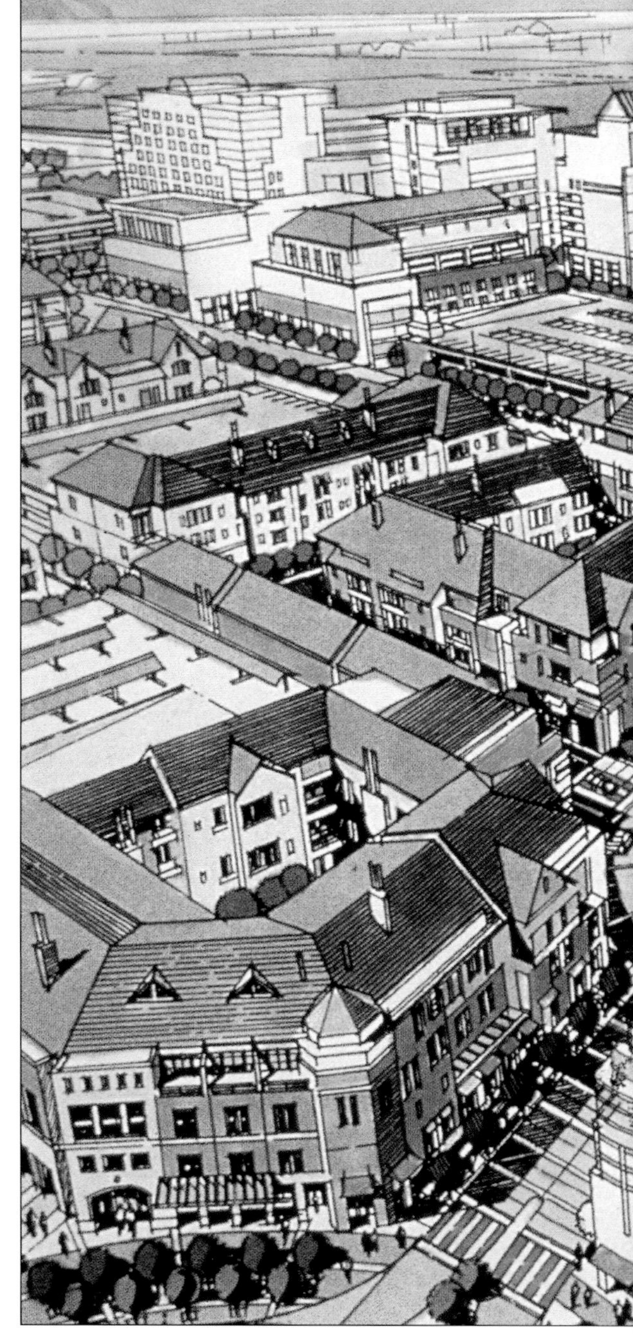

cases are paved in brick, with mature shade trees planted at 25-foot intervals. Larger specimens (in 200-gallon containers) were planted at the outset to provide an instant maturity to the streetscape. Decorative metal guards, similar to those found in English gardens, define the edges of the tree wells. Bike racks, benches, litter containers, and other street furniture add to the usability of the pedestrian-friendly public space.

Both the architecture and site planning contribute to the urban texture of Addison Circle. Most residential buildings are four stories in height; in some cases, three residential levels are located above a ground-floor level of shops and small service businesses. The building designs are modern, but they are domesticated by balconies and bays, gables and brick. Typically, the residential buildings have a stone base course, topped by a red brick facade. Contrasting brick color bands introduce a variety of detail to the finish. Similarly, window elements are used to create architectural diversity; several window types are employed, including large bay window structures painted to contrast with the brickwork. Facades are further articulated with cast stone sills and lintels, dark-green painted metal balconies, and awnings.

Reversing the typical suburban norm of deep building setbacks and narrow sidewalks, the residential building facades at Addison Circle are held close to the street, and sidewalks are generous. Sidewalks are 12 feet deep on residential streets, and buildings are set just six feet back of the sidewalk (18 feet from the curb). The six-foot setback allows for a landscape buffer between sidewalk and building. On boulevards, the sidewalk is 14 feet wide and buildings are set back 24 feet from the curb, allowing for a ten-foot zone for landscaping or outdoor dining.

In form, most residential buildings are doughnut-shaped courtyard buildings. The units are located along both sides of interior corridors with major entries and windows looking out over the street as well as to the interior pool and courtyard areas. The intention of the "full-block closure" building prototype is to avoid functionally ambiguous space: one is either in the public realm, policed by the many windows overlooking the street, or within the security of the building.

Parking is provided in above-grade structures located behind each residential block, allowing residences and shops to open directly onto the street. The structured parking provides for one parking space per bedroom, a ratio that amounts to about 1.4 spaces per dwelling unit.

Secondary auto and pedestrian circulation is provided by "mews"—fire and access lanes located between buildings. The 45-foot right-of-way, paved from building face to building face, consists of two 12-foot vehicular lanes flanked by 10.5-foot-wide sidewalks, defined with street trees but no curbs. Building entries and apartments face out onto the mews, bringing activity to these areas, which also serve as pickup and dropoff points for building residents.

Some apartments open directly out onto several small parks that dot the neighborhood. Low stone walls edge the parks in places, defining pedestrian walkways between park and building. Hiking and bicycling trails are being developed, and a large open space has been dedicated to the town for town-sponsored special events.

A wide range of dwelling unit types are provided at Addison Circle, ranging from 570-square-foot efficiencies that rent for as little as $645 per month to 3,200-square-foot lofts that rent for more than $4,000 a month. While the bulk of units (45 percent) are one-bedroom models, the planned mix also includes two- and three-bedroom units, townhouses, and live/work units.

5

6

7

Most of the residential buildings have both a street face and an inner landscaped courtyard with a pool. All outdoor space is either in full public view—with informal "eyes on the street" surveillance—or within the security of the enclosed courtyard.

8

True to the urban form, entrances open to the street, with a separation created by elevating buildings several steps above the sidewalk.

To a large extent, the market for Addison Circle is an emerging market segment: those who rent by choice, not from necessity. As Paris Rutherford, vice president and director of urban design for RTKL/Dallas notes, "They are largely double-income couples ranging in age from 30 to 55: a mix of young childless professionals and empty nesters. They rent by choice, preferring the urban lifestyle Addison Circle affords."

For this market segment, quality of life is a key issue. Developers like Post Properties are finding that amenities such as pools and health clubs are a starting point, but that for many renters, the idea of a community—everything from having a dry cleaners downstairs, to a

8

coffee bar, to a secure and attractive place in which to stroll or sit—is an increasingly sought-after amenity. "The success of Addison Circle," notes Art Lomenick, executive vice president for development at Post Properties, "is directly tied to an informal sociability created by the mixed-use development pattern."

Addison Circle is being developed in phases. The first phase, including 460 dwelling units, 20,000 square feet of retail, and a half-acre park, was completed in 1997. A second phase, with 610 units, 90,000 square feet of retail, 41,000 square feet of office space, and a 1.5-acre park will be completed in 1999. A total of eight phases are planned, with an expected buildout around 2003 to 2005. Although Post Properties focuses on developing rental projects, a small number of for-sale units is planned for Addison Circle, including 26 in the second phase.

Within the large-scale commercial portion of Addison Circle, one high-rise office building and a mixed-use mid-rise building have been completed. The remaining phases of this sector of Addison Circle are expected to include corporate housing and other residential uses, and office and retail space, ultimately creating some 10,000 permanent jobs.

To develop a project like Addison Circle—radically different and more dense than typical suburban rental projects—the developer had to undertake a series of steps to educate the city and the public to the benefits of the design and to establish the terms of the public/private partnership. In addition to the more usual public workshops, the educational process went so far as to have city staff travel to Chicago and Boston to observe and measure streets and setbacks in several universally admired older urban neighborhoods.

Eventually a set of design and development standards was hammered out with the town and codified in a planned development district approval, covering such items as density, lot coverage, exterior building materials, setbacks, and street landscape standards. Working with town staff, the developer evaluated phasing and development options and their likely impacts on municipal operating and capital budgets. The developer also identified funding gaps that needed to be resolved in order to provide the infrastructure and level of quality mutually desired by the town and the developer.

The final agreement with the town of Addison committed the town to spending $9.5 million out of its general funds over the life of the project: $5.5 million on upfront infrastructure, street, and public open space improvements, and the remaining $4 million in the second phase of development. As Lomenick concludes, "It cost an awful lot of money to build Addison, but unlike some other developments, Addison Circle will be there 100 years from now."

case study

addison circle

addison, texas

land use information

Site Area:	80 acres
Total Dwelling Units:	3,000
Gross Project Density:	37.5 units per acre
Housing Types:	Rental: apartments, townhouses, lofts, corporate suites For-sale: townhouses
Gross Residential Density:	54.6 units per acre
Parking Ratio:	1 space/bdrm
Project Completion Date:	Phase I: 1997 Phase II: 1999 Phase III: 1999 (construction started)
Buildout:	2003–2005 (estimated)

land use plan

	Acres	Percentage of Site
Residential	39	48.8%
Roads/Parking	16	20.0%
Open Space	10	12.5%
Other (public parks)	15	18.7%
Total	80	100.0%

9
To improve the streetscape, parking is located in above-grade structures behind each residential block.

unit information (phases I and II)

Unit Type	Floor Area (Square Feet)	Number Built (Percentage of Total 1,070 Units[1])	Current Rents
Efficiency	570–772	20%	$645–$786
1-bdrm	681–1,079	45%	$800–$1,220
2-bdrm	870–1,521	19%	$1,013–$2,015
3-bdrm	1,507	1%	$1,591
Lofts	807–3,219	16%	$870–$4,400

[1]Phases I and II only.

contact information

Developer	Post Properties, Inc. 4401 Northside Parkway Suite 800 Atlanta, Georgia 30327 404-846-5000
Architect and Master Planner	RTKL Associates, Inc. 2828 Routh Street, Suite 200 Dallas, Texas 75201 214-871-8877
Engineer and Landscape Architect	Huit-Zollars 3131 McKinney Avenue Dallas, Texas 75204 214-871-3311

case study

The Oriental Warehouse

San Francisco, California

The view from the northwest corner tells the story in a glimpse: out of the eroded walls of an old brick warehouse has arisen a modern condominium structure of white-painted steel and glass. "21st-century housing in a 19th-century shell" is how principal Rodney Friedman of Fisher-Friedman Architects describes the 66-unit loft project in San Francisco's South Beach neighborhood.

In its current incarnation, the brick walls of the warehouse have been stabilized and a new structure built—from the ground up—within the century-old perimeter. The two-story live/work dwelling units, stacked two high over ground-floor parking, look out through big picture windows to airy light courts, which fill the void between the original brick exterior walls and the new structure.

The Oriental Warehouse originally was constructed in 1868 to serve the city's expanding Asia trade. At that time, it was a waterfront site. Later, the structure is believed to have been used as a processing center for Asian immigrants. Owned for many years by the Southern Pacific Railroad, the building passed through several developer ownerships from 1980 until it was purchased by the Reliance Development Group of New York in 1987.

Although it survived the great 1906 earthquake, the brick and timber warehouse was nearly felled by a series of fires and earthquakes between 1988 and 1994. The first event, an arson fire, destroyed much of the timber framing of the south bay of the three-bay structure. The following year, in 1989, the warehouse was rocked by the Loma Prieta earthquake, which opened a series of cracks in the brick shell. And, in a reprise of the earlier damage, a second fire—also attributed to arson—ravaged the north side of the warehouse in 1994, resulting in the partial collapse of the north and east walls of the structure.

After the second fire, all that remained of the warehouse were the exterior brick walls—partially destroyed—and the center bay of timber framing. At this point, the existing renovation plans were scrapped and a new vision—that of a new freestanding building within the old building—was born.

1
2

Note: Images for this case study are courtesy of Fisher-Friedman Associates.

1, 2, 3

The brick skin of the original warehouse peeled away, revealing a new, modern, freestanding steel and glass structure within. The new construction houses 66 two-story live/work units with 90 garage parking spaces.

4

Building section shows the original warehouse structure and the renovation with light courts between the three bays of apartments.

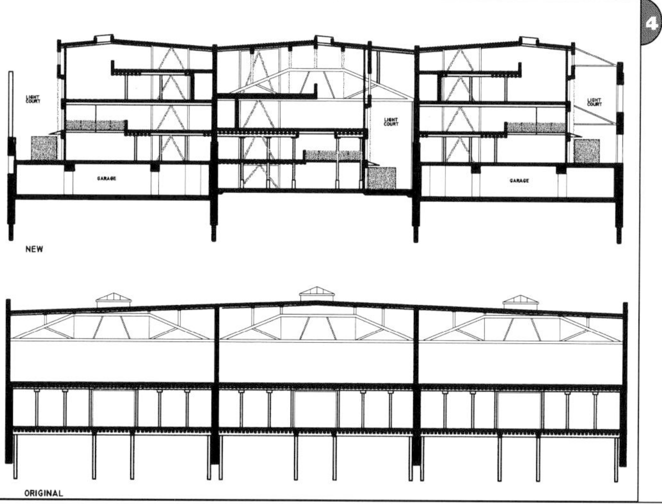

5, 6

Old brick contrasts with polished stainless steel and glass at the entrance of the Oriental Warehouse. While the concept mixes old and new, it retains the industrial character of the building.

7

Three bays of apartment units are built within the stabilized walls of the old warehouse. Air and light are provided by the light courts—open space between the original walls and the new construction as well as between the center and end bays.

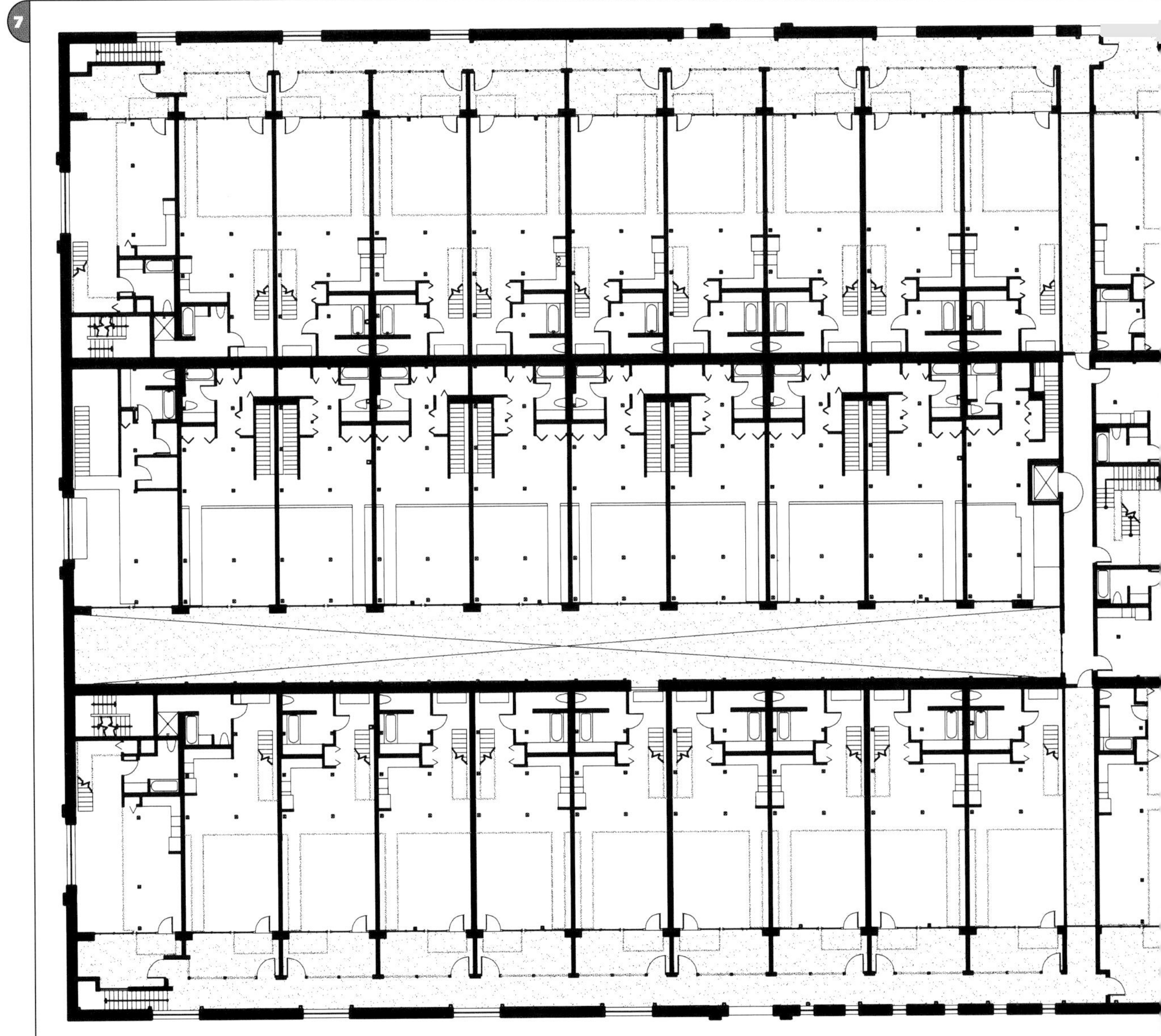

As developed, the Oriental Warehouse's 66 dwelling units are laid out in three 65-foot by 200-foot rows, corresponding to the original three bays of the warehouse. Parking fills the north and south bays at the ground floor. A single row of dwellings in the center bay is accessed by a skylit "mews." Ninety parking spaces were provided, a ratio of 1.36 spaces per dwelling unit. Because most households today have two cars, second parking spaces (limited in number) proved to be in high demand and commanded a premium price.

At the first floor, above the parking, the units in the north and south bays are set back from the original exterior brick wall, creating the light courts. The 15-foot-wide setback, open to the sky, allows for a nine-foot row of patios, which mediates between the access walkway and the individual dwelling units. Large square openings were cut in the north and south brick walls to brighten the light courts, a measure that required extensive deliberation by the landmarks commission and provoked considerable controversy in preservation-minded San Francisco.

The new building, in marked contrast with the old, is framed in steel and finished in painted corrugated sheet metal. Heavy steel bracing, designed to echo the original timber trusswork, provides seismic support for the unreinforced brick walls, which have been cleaned and repaired.

New black anodized, multipane aluminum windows were inserted in the existing arched window openings, providing a modern contrast to the weathered brick. Similarly, 12-foot-high stainless steel doors with glass surrounds were set into an existing loading dock opening to serve as the building entrance. Beyond the monumental doors, the lobby stairway is a high-tech assemblage of stainless steel, cable, and glass.

The dwelling units blend modernist imagery with timber details reminiscent of the original warehouse construction. The units, which range in size from 1,300 to 1,700 square feet, typically are 20 feet wide and have 17-foot-high living room ceilings. The floors are oak, the walls are a smooth-finished drywall (and in some cases brick or exposed concrete), and the ceilings are exposed steel decking. The structural steel columns and beams framing the building are similarly exposed, as is the timber framing used to support sleeping loft mezzanines. In addition, the original wood roof trusses of the center bay were incorporated into the design of the dwelling units.

8

The warehouse's original brick walls remain largely for aesthetic purposes. Because so much damage had occurred over the years, their functional use could no longer be retained, but they were preserved for their historic value and the sense of place they instill.

9

10

All the dwelling units feature one-bedroom lofts and two baths. Two of the units, facing the front of the building, are four stories, and the top units in the center bay are three stories (two stories in a three-story volume).

Construction of the Oriental Warehouse condominium project was self-financed by the developer, Reliance Development Group. The project is actually one piece of a larger effort being undertaken by Reliance. The developer has approvals for 356 units of high-rise condominium housing to be built in three 17-story towers adjacent to the Oriental Warehouse. One hundred thirty of these units are now under construction. As part of a negotiated package, Reliance was granted a density transfer, allowing the developer to add 50 feet of height to the high-rise portion of the project in return for undertaking the Oriental Warehouse renovation.

The Oriental's residential units were released for sale in three phases, corresponding to the three rows of units, with the center bay held for last. Initial prices were set in the low $300,000 range, with price increases as each successive group of units was released. Sales averaged 5.5 units per month. Buyers were a combination of young professionals—some with children—and empty nesters. In the two years since completion, resale prices have skyrocketed, increasing 75 percent in some cases to reach the mid-$600,000 range.

The Oriental Warehouse is a striking marriage of modern design and historic preservation. The project has dealt with the issue of integrating new construction with the old by designing the new work as a visual counterpoint to the existing historic elements. In so doing, the project has clearly highlighted, and preserved, the historic qualities of the structure.

The novelty of constructing a new building within an old building—dictated in this case by necessity—has caught on with San Francisco buyers, who seem to find the unique juxtaposition of the modern design and the old brick particularly appealing in this age of standardized housing choices. The two-story loft designs have stimulated wide market interest. Intended as live/work units, the lofts have attracted not only artists or those with home-based businesses but also a wide audience that appreciates the generous spatial qualities afforded by the design.

9, 10

The space between the old brick factory walls and the new corrugated sheet metal apartment walls allows light and air to enter the apartments.

11

A lobby staircase shows the elegance of raw industrial materials.

12

Typical unit plans.

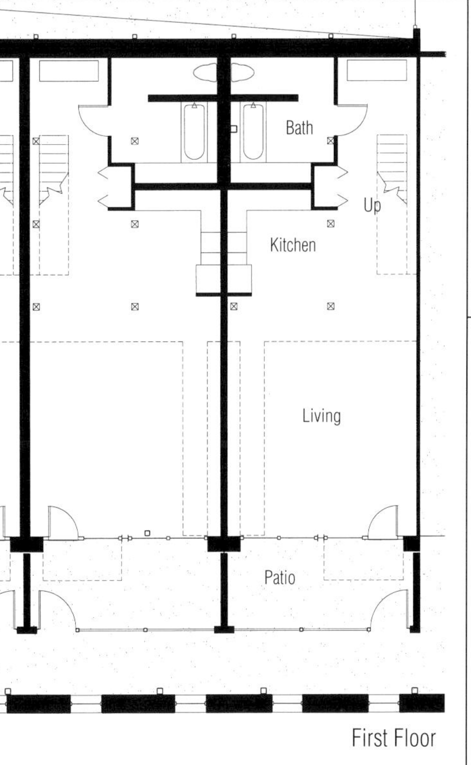

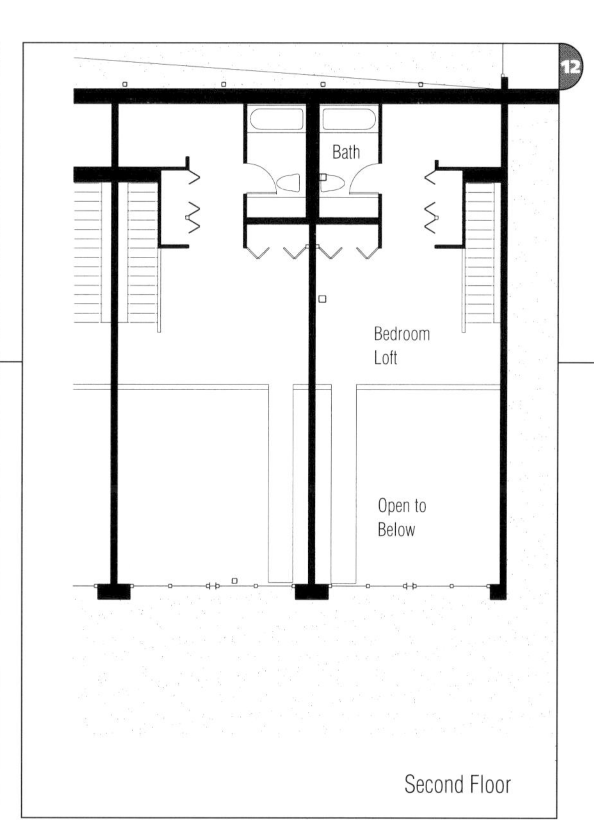

case study

the oriental warehouse

san francisco, california

land use information

Site Area:	1.49 acres
Total Dwelling Units:	66
Gross Project Density:	44.3 units per acre
Housing Type:	Lofts (live/work)
Gross Residential Density:	63.5 units per acre
Parking, Total:	90 spaces
Parking Ratio:	1.36 spaces/unit
Project Completion Date:	February 1996

land use plan

	Acres	Percentage of Site
Residential	1.03	69%
Roads/Parking	0.10	7%
Open Space	0.36	24%
Total	1.49	100%

13

13, 14

The industrial theme is carried into the residential units, but with plenty of polish. Wood beams, corrugated metal ceilings, and exposed ductwork meld with glossy wood floors and smooth-finished drywall.

15

The center bay of apartment units is made possible by light courts that allow air and light into the units from above.

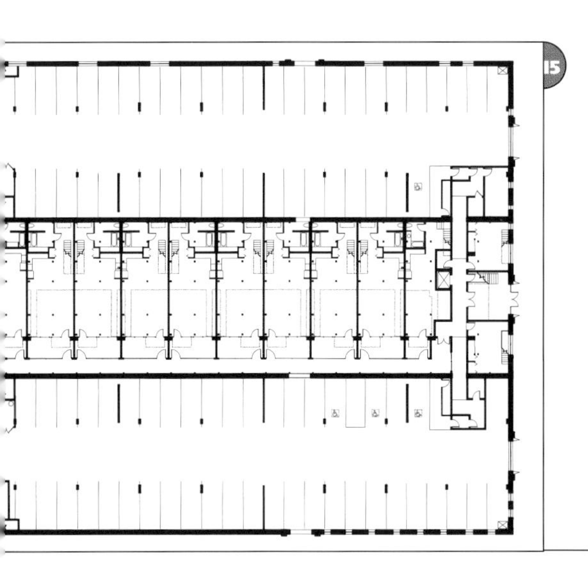

development costs

	Total	Cost per Dwelling Unit	Cost per Residential Square Foot
Site Acquisition Cost	$2,424,100[1]	$36,729	$25.68
Construction Cost	$16,672,800	$252,618	$176.62
Soft Costs	$2,337,000	$35,409	$24.76
Total Development Cost	$21,433,900	$324,756	$227.06

unit information

Unit Type	Floor Area (Square Feet)	Number	Final Sales Prices
Basic loft	1,400	54	$327,000
End loft	1,600	10	$350,000
3-story loft	1,400	2	$350,000
Total		66	

[1]Allocated.

contact information

Developer	Reliance Development Group 55 East 52nd Street New York, New York 10055 212-909-130
Design Architect	Fisher-Friedman Associates 333 Bryant Street, Suite 200 San Francisco, California 94107 415-981-6076
Associated Architect	Loving and Campos Architects, Inc. 245 Ygnacio Valley Road Walnut Creek, California 94596 925-944-1626

case study

courthouse Hill

Arlington, Virginia

Courthouse Hill is a 202-unit infill project of townhouses and mid-rise condominiums located in Arlington, Virginia, just one block from the Courthouse Station of the Washington, D.C., Metrorail. Although the project is surrounded by a mix of high-rise offices and residential buildings, as well as low-rise housing to the south, the developer, Eakin/Youngentob Associates, avoided the tower-in-the-park solution for which the 4.6-acre site was zoned. Instead, inspired by the 18th- and 19th-century rowhouse neighborhoods of the Washington area, the developer focused on creating a pedestrian-oriented neighborhood, taking advantage of the urban context of the site.

The result is a project of 69 three-story townhomes and 133 condominiums in a mix of four-, five-, and six-story structures, woven together by a network of landscaped parks and pathways. At 29 units per acre for the townhouses, and 87 for the condominiums, the project has achieved densities greater than those usually reached by comparable projects. At the same time, because of the high level of building and site detailing—everything from tree-lined brick walkways to molded cornices—the project sold out rapidly and commanded above-average per-square-foot prices.

The Courthouse Hill site was a difficult one; the area was urban, yet not particularly friendly to pedestrians. Sloping 35 feet from end to end, the site bordered high rises on one side and single-family residences on the other. Although well located, the cleared site had remained vacant for ten years before Eakin/Youngentob purchased it.

To Eakin/Youngentob Associates, the high-rise idea was exactly the opposite of what the site needed. What was required, the developer and architect reasoned, was a greater connectedness to the site's context, not the lesser engagement implied by high-rise development. What was needed was the reestablishment of the urban pattern and a pedestrian scale. Notes architect Chris Lessard, principal of Lessard Architectural Group, "At over five stories up, people start to feel disconnected from the street level." The low/mid-rise solu-

1

Lessard Architectural Group

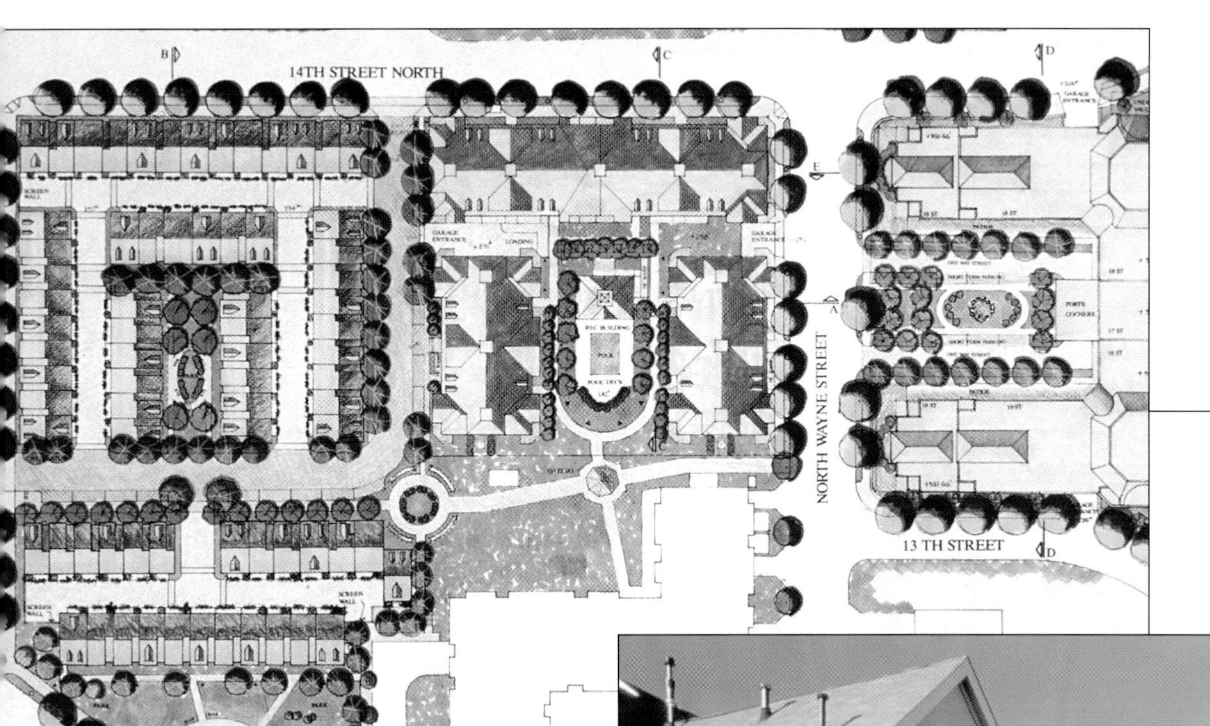

2

1

Carefully placed green space alleviates Courthouse Hill's dense urban plan. Some townhouses face public parks; others cluster around small private gardens.

2

Site plan.

3

Condominium building fronts are close to the street. Their backs overlook a courtyard with a pool and a recreation building.

Lessard Architectural Group

3

Eakin/Youngentob Associates

4

tion would also provide a much-needed break in the skyline, and it would not block light and sun from the surrounding streets.

As a first step in integrating the project within its context, the decision was made to bridge the differences in massing of the surrounding structures. Lessard notes, "The layout of housing units on the site sought to create a 'layering effect' that tied the project into the neighborhood." This was achieved by stepping down in height from the high-rise office/retail center and Metro to the north to the low-rise housing to the south. The taller condominium buildings step from six to five to four stories, and the townhomes complete the layering effect by establishing a three-story profile adjacent to the community park and existing residential neighborhood to the south.

A second element in the pedestrian-oriented design strategy was placing the building entrances on the street and relegating parking to the interior of the site. Borrowing from 18th- and 19th-century town models, the Courthouse Hill structures are set close to the street, just 14.5-feet from the curb. Entrances to the individual townhouses are raised, both for privacy and to accommodate tucked-under parking.

Each townhouse has a lower-level two-car garage, accessed via an interior driveway. Parking for the condominium buildings is provided in below-grade structures. To deal with the 35-foot elevation gradient of the site, the interior of the site was regraded, allowing for relatively level driveways. Along with the regrading, the garage level of some of the townhouses was set partially below grade.

The configuration of open space is another component of the project's design that helps to establish a pedestrian orientation. A one-half-acre public park was constructed on the southern edge of the project, providing a linkage to the recreation center across the street and the neighborhood beyond. Landscaped pathways thread their way from the park through Courthouse Hill, connecting to the Metro and the urban core to the north. These walkways are pledged to public use through a pedestrian access easement.

Other open spaces are more private, serving as quiet courtyards or recreation areas for residents of the townhouses and condominiums. Tucked within the U shape of the condominium buildings is a swimming pool and a community center that includes an exercise room, a multipurpose room, and bathhouse facilities. Sidewalks at Courthouse Hill, as well as internal walkways, are paved in brick. Lanterns and period streetlights illuminate both sidewalks and internal walkways, further recalling the project's urban antecedents.

Eakin/Youngentob Associates

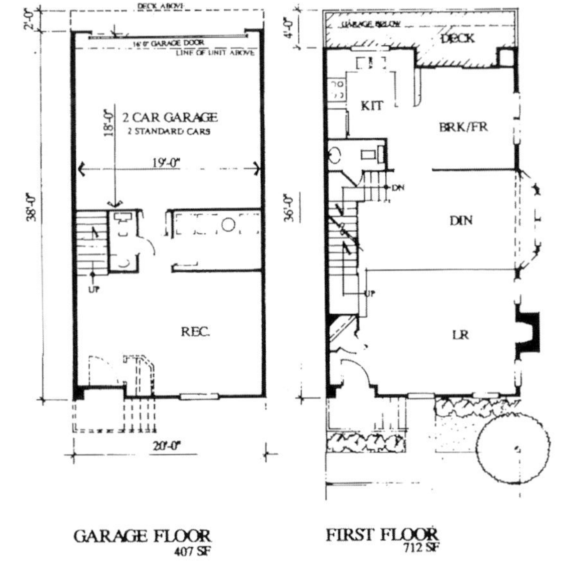

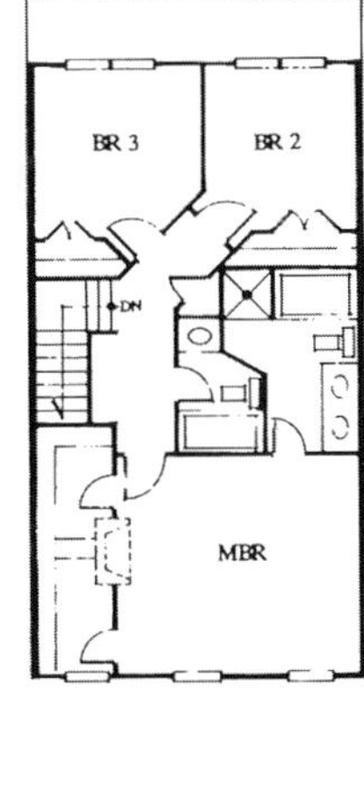

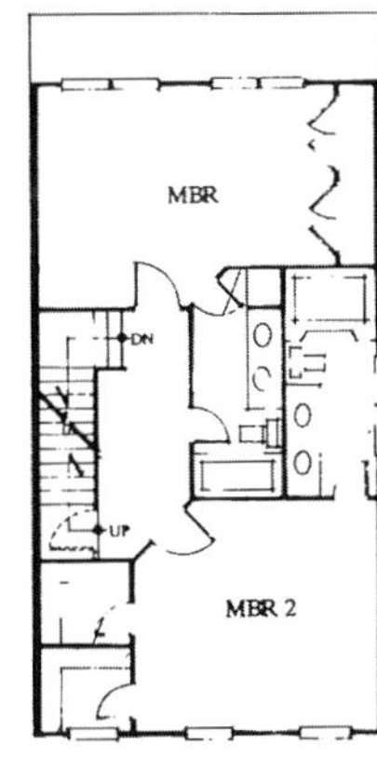

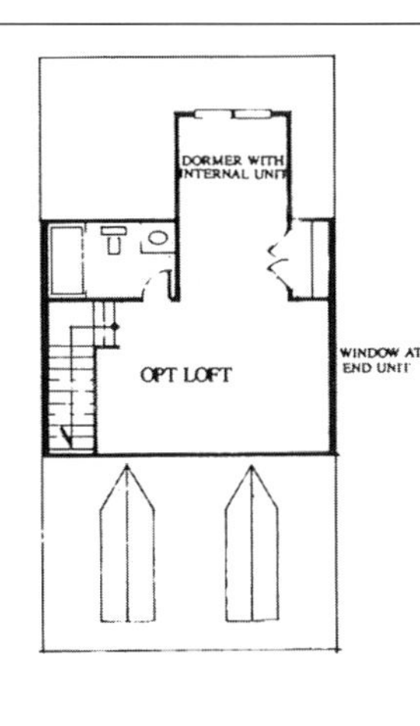

Although built all of a piece by one developer, the townhouse facades at Courthouse Hill are varied, echoing the eclectic mix typical of older neighborhoods built one house at a time. The highly detailed brick facades are federalist in style, with pedimented doorways, arched window heads, and strong cornice lines. Dormer windows punctuate the steeply pitched roofs. At the street level, raised entry stoops with metal railings provide a rhythm and a unifying element to the facades.

The lowest level of the townhouse units includes a recreation room as well as a laundry room and the garage. The main living quarters are located one floor above, with bedrooms on the third level. An additional loft/bedroom

4

The mid-rise condominium buildings encircle the project's pool and recreation building, all of which are built atop the underground parking garage.

5

Because of steep slopes, Courthouse Hill's 4.6-acre site was a difficult one. Despite its sought-after urban location, it sat vacant for ten years awaiting a purchaser. Eakin/Youngentob worked out a site plan that makes appropriate use of the terrain and ties the project to its urban context.

6

Typical townhouse floor plan.

is offered as a buyer option, above the primary bedroom level, under the standard roofline.

The condominium buildings are a less literal translation of period architecture, but employ the same finishes as the townhouses. As with the townhouses, the elevations are highly articulated, with painted wood details contrasting with the brick facades. Recessed balconies further modulate the elevations. Roofs are pitched and accented with dormers and gables of varying sizes.

The market response to Courthouse Hill was very positive. Nearly all of the 204 units were sold in less than 18 months, a rate of about 11 units per month. Prices ranged from $115,000 to $280,000 for the condominiums, while the townhomes ranged from $280,000 to $350,000. Twenty-eight of the 133 condominium units were designated as affordable for-sale housing, fulfilling county requirements for the project.

At Courthouse Hill, Eakin/Youngentob Associates sought to take advantage of its urban location. The proximity to urban amenities was a major selling point to potential residents who placed a high value on being within walking distance to mass transit, restaurants, movie theaters, shops, and offices. According to architect Lessard, "We were trying to appeal to the young person or the empty nester who is interested in a vibrant street life. So in our design we sought to create a sense of community that related to and enhanced the surrounding urban environment." Adds developer Bob Youngentob, "Our target market was not people who want to live in a gated community, but people who want to feel a part of a neighborhood."

7

Lessard Architectural Group

Lessard Architectural Group

7, 8

Both the townhouses and condominiums draw on the local colonial architecture. But the condominiums are loose interpretations, as befits a modern product type, while the townhouses replicate historic houses of nearby neighborhoods.

9

Typical condominium floor plans.

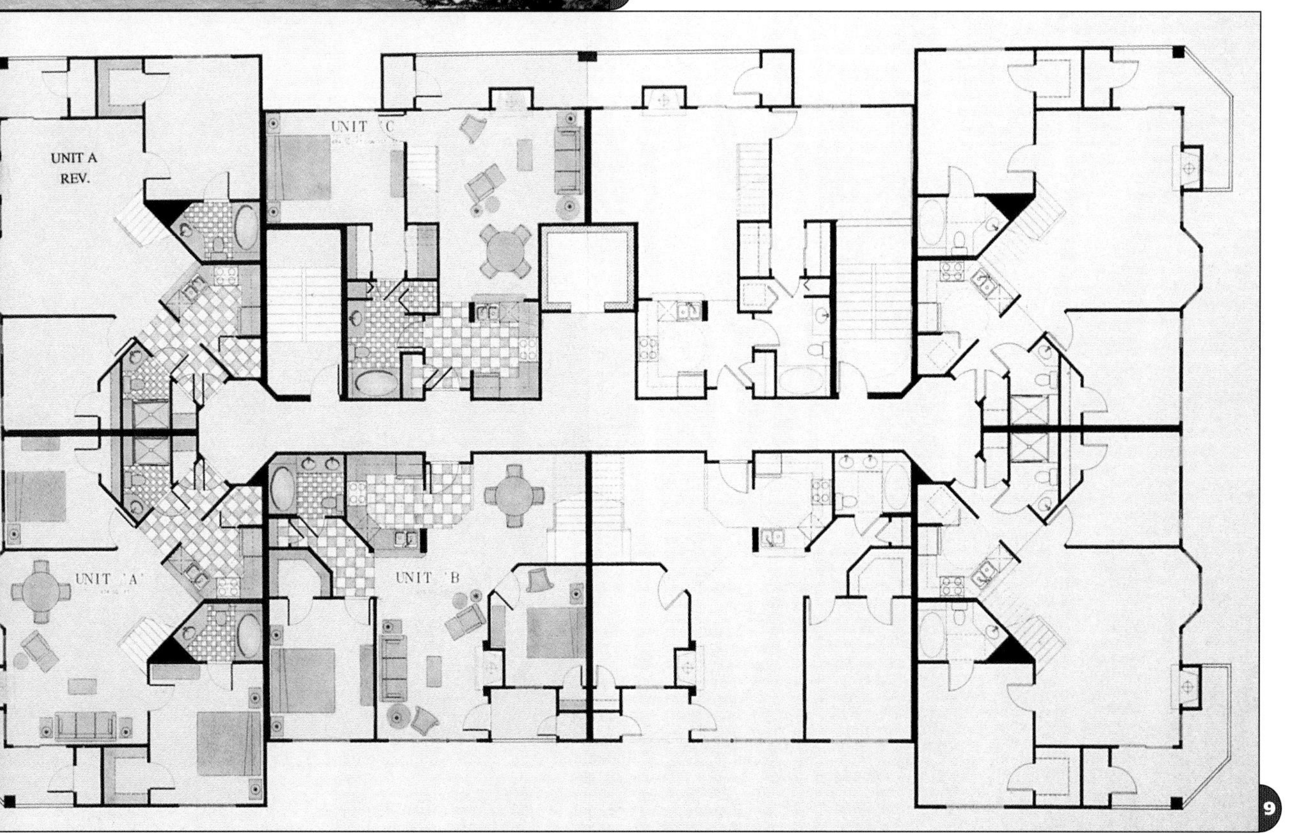

case study

courthouse Hill

arlington, virginia

land use information

Site Area:	4.6 acres
Total Dwelling Units:	202
Gross Project Density:	43.9 units per acre
Housing Types:	Townhouses (69) and condominiums (133)
Average Lot Size:	902 square feet
Gross Residential Density:	69.7 units per acre
Parking, Total:	345 spaces
Parking Ratio:	1.71 spaces/unit
Project Completion Date:	April 1997

land use plan

	Acres	Percentage of Site
Residential	2.1	46%
Recreation/Amenities	0.7	15%
Roads/Parking	0.8	17%
Open Space	1.0	22%
Total	4.6	100%

Lessard Architectural Group

10

An aerial view of the project shows how stepping down building heights relates the infill project to both high-rise and single-family neighbors, unifying the once-disjointed neighborhood.

unit information

Unit Type	Floor Area (Square Feet)	Number Planned	Final Sales Prices
1-bdrm condo	733	45	$115,000–$125,000
2-bdrm condo	700–1,100	68	$140,000–$205,000
3-bdrm condo	1,267	20	$220,000–$280,000
2-bdrm + loft/2 1/2-bath townhouse[1]	2,076	37	$280,000–$330,000
2-bdrm + loft/2 1/2-bath townhouse[1]	2,100	32	$320,000–$350,000
Total		202	

[1]Optional third bedroom and bath in lieu of loft.

contact information

Developer	Eakin/Youngentob Associates 1000 Wilson Boulevard, Suite 2720 Arlington, Virginia 22209 703-525-5565
Architect	The Lessard Architectural Group 8603 Westwood Center Drive Suite 400 Vienna, Virginia 22182 703-760-9344
Landscape Architect	Studio 39 Landscape Architecture 6416 Grovedale Drive Suite 100A Alexandria, Virginia 22310 703-719-6500

case study

paseo plaza

san jose, california

Paseo Plaza represents a hybrid housing form: two-level townhouses at the street level, with stacked condominium apartments above. The 210-unit condominium project, located in downtown San Jose, is part of the city's ongoing redevelopment program. Its neighbors are the recently constructed San Jose Repertory Theatre, and the San Jose Museum of Art, as well as San Jose State University, which borders the project to the east. The first two phases of Paseo Plaza were completed in 1997 and 1998, respectively. A third phase of 104 units is under construction, with completion expected in April 2000.

From an urban design standpoint, the intention of Paseo Plaza's scheme is to engage the street, rather than turn defensively inward, as many new urban projects do. Thus, the mid-rise development has a strong public orientation, as well as a more private interior core. The townhouses—each with its own street entrance—line the Third and Fourth street frontages of the development, while retail storefronts edge the Paseo Mall, a pedestrian walkway that forms the southern boundary of the project. The townhouses are set back only five feet from the sidewalk along Third Street and 12 feet along Fourth Street.

Stacked above the townhouses are single-story condominium units: four stories of flats along Third and Fourth streets and three levels above the townhouses that line the "mews"—an internal pedestrian "street." Along the Paseo, three-story townhouses top the first-floor shops.

Parking is located in a below-grade structure, the top of which forms a podium for the townhouses and for the project's landscaped courtyards. In addition to the multiple street entries to the individual townhouses, a primary canopy-covered building entry is located on the Third Street side. A second, less formal building entry is provided on the opposite (Fourth Street) side.

1

Note: Images for this case study are courtesy of Backen Arrigoni & Ross/Douglas Dun.

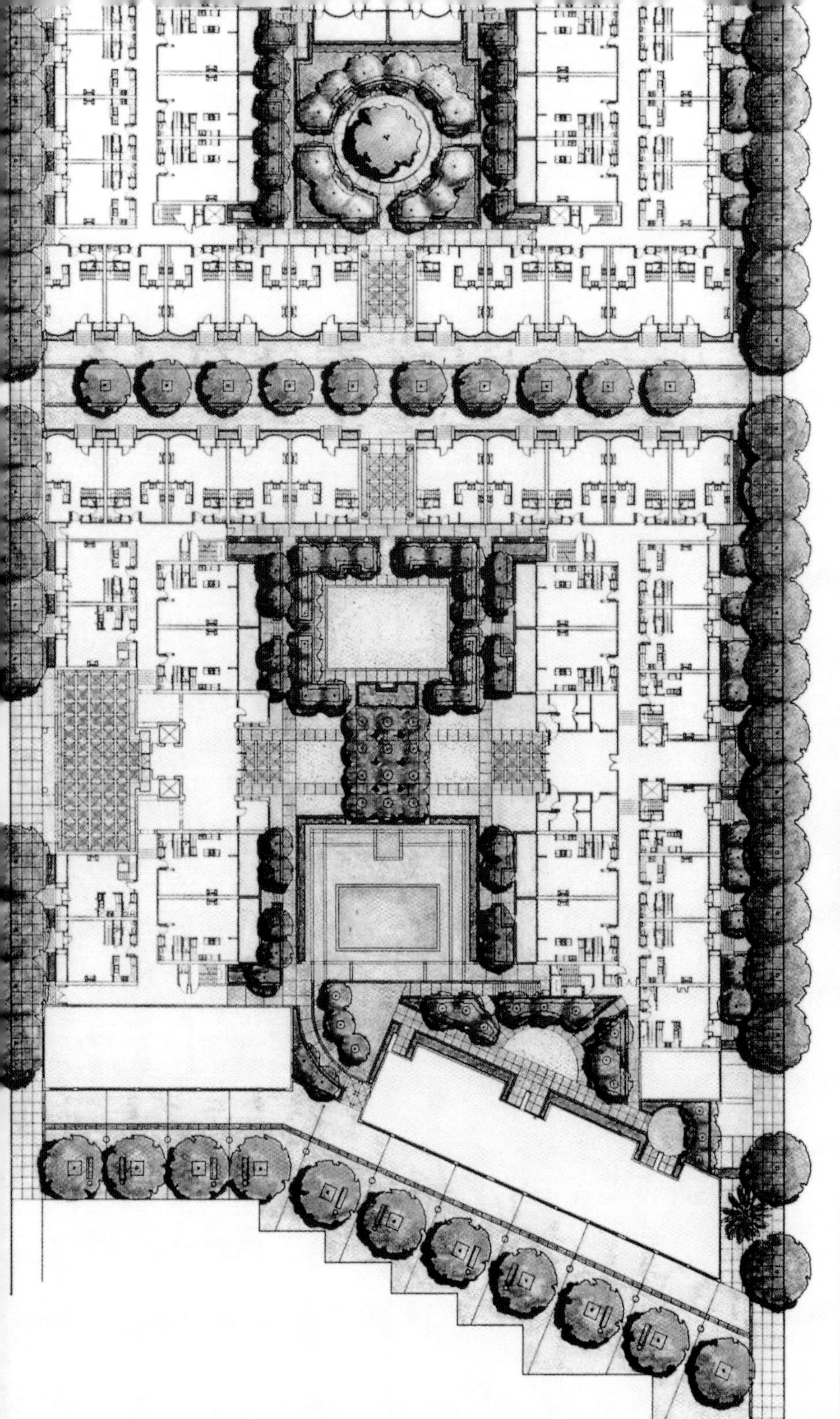

1

Paseo Plaza encourages a more urban, pedestrian-oriented ambience with its human scale and entrances on the street. Facades are richly detailed, featuring bay windows, recessed balconies, and traditional front stoops.

2

The plan incorporates a range of outdoor spaces: public sidewalks, a pedestrian walkway lined with retail shops, the mews, and the recreational courtyards.

3

Interior mews with apartment entrances.

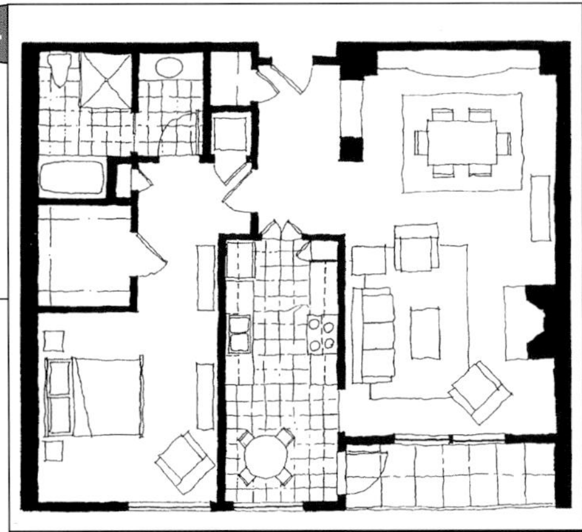

Both entries open onto the main courtyard, a large open space that is differentiated into three smaller areas: a pool terrace, a lawn terrace, and the central paved terrace. A second courtyard, more intimate in scale, has the feeling of a private garden. Linking the two courtyards is a barrel-vaulted walkway that passes through the residential structures on either side of the mews. A recreation room is also located on the podium level, the roof of which serves as a landscaped forecourt for the townhouses overlooking the Paseo.

At the street level, the design of Paseo Plaza "draws on the inspiration of Boston's Back Bay townhouses and the Georgian terrace housing in England," notes Bruce Ross, principal of Backen Arrigoni & Ross, Inc. (BAR), the project's design architect. The two-story townhouse portion of the facade is sheathed in a light-colored stucco, scored to recall coursed stone. Projecting stoops and planter boxes, as well as the deeply inset townhouse entries, add articulation to the facade. The townhouse entries are raised a half-flight to accommodate the partially subterranean garage as well as to increase the sense of privacy for residents. Decorative flower pots and closely spaced street trees further enliven the perspective at the street level.

Above, the condominium flats are clad in an ocher-colored stucco, to contrast with the "stone" of the townhouse facades below. Balconies are recessed five feet from the principal plane of the facade and are grouped together, establishing a rhythm of alternating "in" and "out" planes that breaks up the bulk of the nearly 400-foot-long project. Through this device, the building begins to recall the sense of individual urban structures. The detailing of the building—dark green–painted metal windows and balcony railings, as well as cast-concrete sills and trim—ties the upper and lower sections of the facade together into a unified composition.

Along Third and Fourth streets, both the townhouses and flats are double-loaded along hallways, with units looking out over the street and units looking into the courtyards. Townhouses facing the courtyard have private patios. Along the mews, both townhouses and flats are single-loaded. Typically, the flats are 48 feet wide and sited directly above pairs of townhouses, each 24 feet wide.

The mews is an intimate space, gated at both ends. The pedestrians-only street spans 40 feet from building face to building face. The actual pedestrian walkway is 15 feet wide, lined with ornamental pear trees and decorative street lamps. Private townhouse patios, 12.5 feet deep, flank the walkway on either side.

Paseo's townhouses have two or three bedrooms and range in size from 1,390 square feet to about 2,200 square feet.

4

Typical floor plan for one-bedroom flat with 1,110 square feet.

5

First-floor retail space at the south end of the project faces existing first-floor retail, thus enclosing the public pedestrian area with activity generators.

6

While the project opens its arms to the street, a hierarchy of privacy is established—from the very public sidewalk entries, to the semipublic mews entries and finally to the private courtyards.

7

Building section.

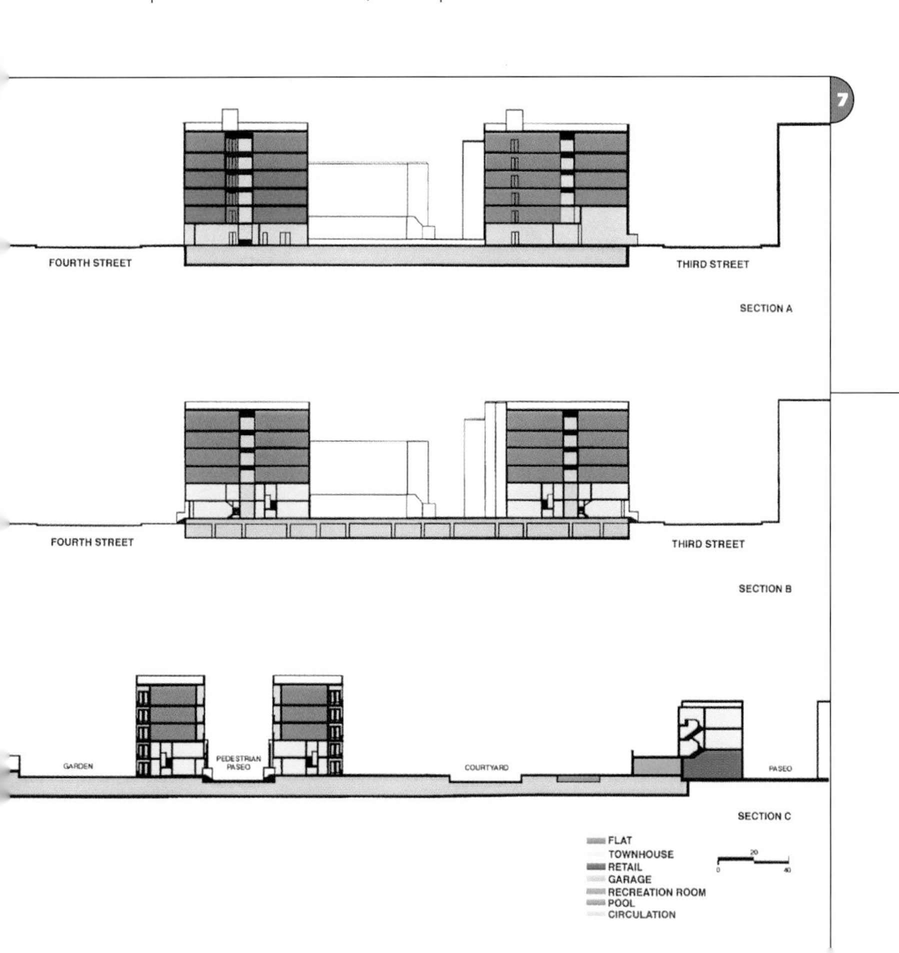

Some of the models have large bay windows, and others have double-height living rooms or bedrooms. The townhouse units originally sold at prices ranging from the low $200,000s to approximately $500,000.

The flats were targeted to a lower price range. The one- and two-bedroom units, which range in size from 847 square feet to 1,450 square feet, were priced from $165,000 to about $300,000. With an eye toward affordability, the two-bedroom flats were designed as "double masters," with two equally sized,

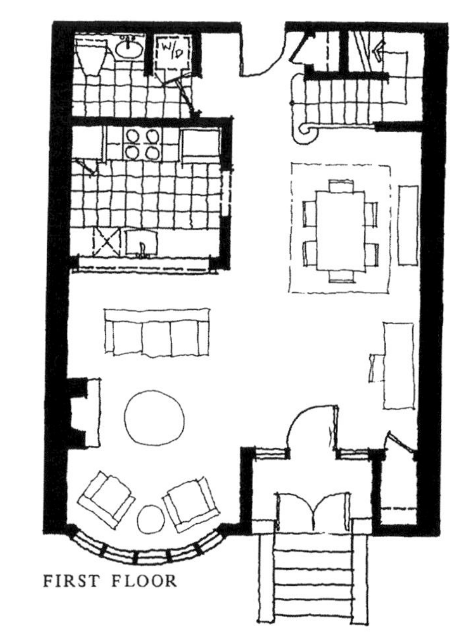

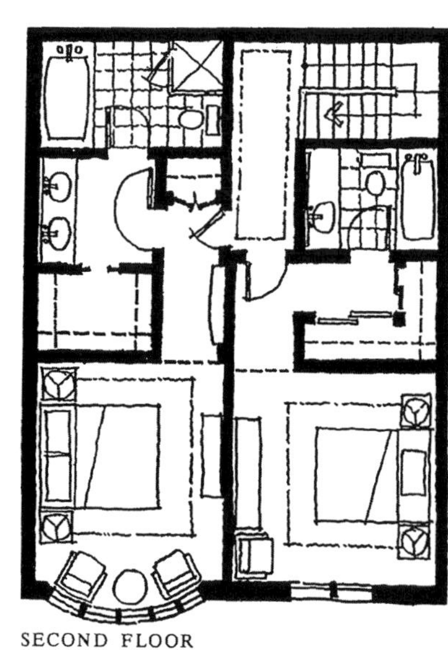

8, 10

The private interior courtyard includes a pool and landscaped areas where residents may congregate.

9

Typical floor plan for two-story, two-bedroom townhouse.

10

mirror-image bedroom/bathroom suites that could be marketed to two unrelated singles pooling their resources. The flats have nine-foot ceilings.

The sales program for Paseo Plaza, which lasted approximately 30 months, averaged about seven units per month over the full duration. The townhouses, with their entries on the street and their higher prices, were more of a pioneering effort for downtown San Jose; they sold more slowly than the more affordable flats. Sales for all units increased considerably in the final 12 months, however, as the project became established, and resales are realizing gains on the order of 25 percent in just the past year.

Paseo's retail space has been less successful to date, and several of the storefronts remain vacant. However, development in the area is continuing—with Phase III of Paseo Plaza, as well as other housing and nonresidential projects—and demand for Paseo retail eventually may catch up to supply.

Bruce Ross of BAR architects credits the Redevelopment Agency for the overall success of Paseo Plaza. He notes, "They were like a partner in the deal," programming the site, setting the objectives of a pedestrian-friendly urban environment, and contributing resources, including infrastructure and decorative street lighting. In return, the city has gained an active residential anchor contributing to the rebirth of downtown San Jose.

case study

paseo plaza

san jose, california

land use information

Site Area:	2.86 acres
Total Dwelling Units:	210
Gross Project Density:	73.4 units per acre
Housing Types:	Townhouses and flats
Gross Residential Density:	137.3 units per acre
Parking, Total:	369 spaces
Parking Ratio:	1.76 spaces/unit
Project Completion Date:	1998

land use plan

	Acres	Percentage of Site
Residential	1.53	53.5%
Parking[1]	—	—
Open Space[2]	1.15	40.2%
Other (retail)	0.18	6.3%
Total	2.86	100.0%

[1]Below-grade parking (approximately 124,000 square feet).
[2]Includes outdoor recreation areas.

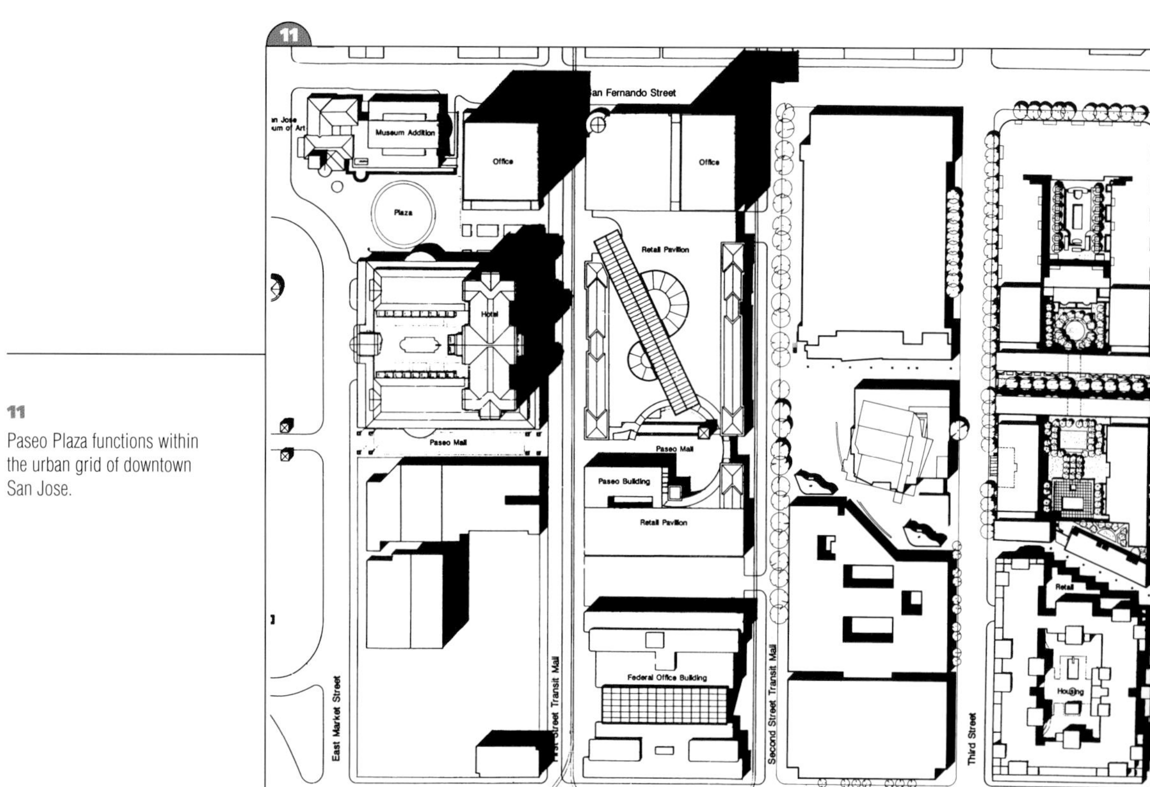

11
Paseo Plaza functions within the urban grid of downtown San Jose.

development costs

	Total	Cost per Dwelling Unit	Cost per Residential Square Foot
Site Acquisition Cost	N/A	N/A	N/A
Site Improvement and Construction Cost	$32,000,000	$152,381	$125
Total Development Cost	$32,000,000	$152,381	$125

unit information

Unit Type	Floor Area (Square Feet)	Number of Units	Final Sales Prices
1-bdrm/1-bath flat	847–1,125	45	$164,900–$209,900
2-bdrm/2-bath flat	1,384–1,483	97	$220,900–$319,900
2-bdrm/2 1/2-bath townhouse	1,316–1,773	60	$264,900–$379,900
3-bdrm/2 1/2-bath townhouse	1,860–2,189	8	$359,900–$499,900
Total		210	

contact information

Developer	Goldrich Kest & Stern One Maritime Plaza San Francisco, California 94111 415-788-5894
Design Architect	Backen Arrigoni & Ross, Inc. 1660 Bush Street San Francisco, California 94109 415-441-4771
Executive Architect	Johannes Van Tilburg & Partners Penthouse, 225 Arizona Avenue Santa Monica, California 90401 310-394-0273
Landscape Architect	Stephen Wheeler 55 New Montgomery San Francisco, California 94105 415-974-5995

case study

The Cotton Mill

New Orleans, Louisiana

In 1882, Ambrose A. Maginnis and Sons began construction of a large textile manufacturing plant in the Warehouse District of New Orleans. Before construction, the site had been occupied by a series of plantations dating back to 1765. By 1884, the mill was fully established, and it remained the largest cotton mill in the South until it ceased operations in 1944. When the HRI Group purchased the property in 1996, the Cotton Mill was vacant except for one small textile manufacturing tenant.

Since then, the Cotton Mill has been rehabilitated and converted into 269 rental apartments, with 18 condominium units constructed on the roof of the existing structure. The massive renovation project was the largest of its kind in New Orleans's Warehouse District and one of the largest in the country. Its presence has injected a welcome dose of activity and vitality into the emerging warehouse/arts district, adjacent to downtown New Orleans.

The 323,000-square-foot Cotton Mill is actually a composite of six three- and four-story structures, which ring the block and enclose a one-half-acre courtyard. The buildings were constructed in the traditional manner, with load-bearing brick exterior walls and a heavy timber system of interior columns and beams. Huge double-hung cypress windows, five feet wide by 12 feet high, rhythmically punctuate the thick exterior skin.

In addition to the primary mill structures, the complex included several smaller structures abutting the main buildings, primarily within the courtyard. A few of these structures, including a transformer vault and an overhead bridge, were removed to open up the courtyard and bring daylight to the courtyard facades. The selective demolition provided space for a swimming pool, a pergola constructed of salvaged metal floor gratings, and a raised concrete "stage" area that sits on the foundation of the removed transformer vault. Within the 25,000-square-foot open space, several smaller, more intimate courtyards and spaces have been created by retaining part of the original brick walls.

1

Note: Images for this case study are courtesy of HRI Group.

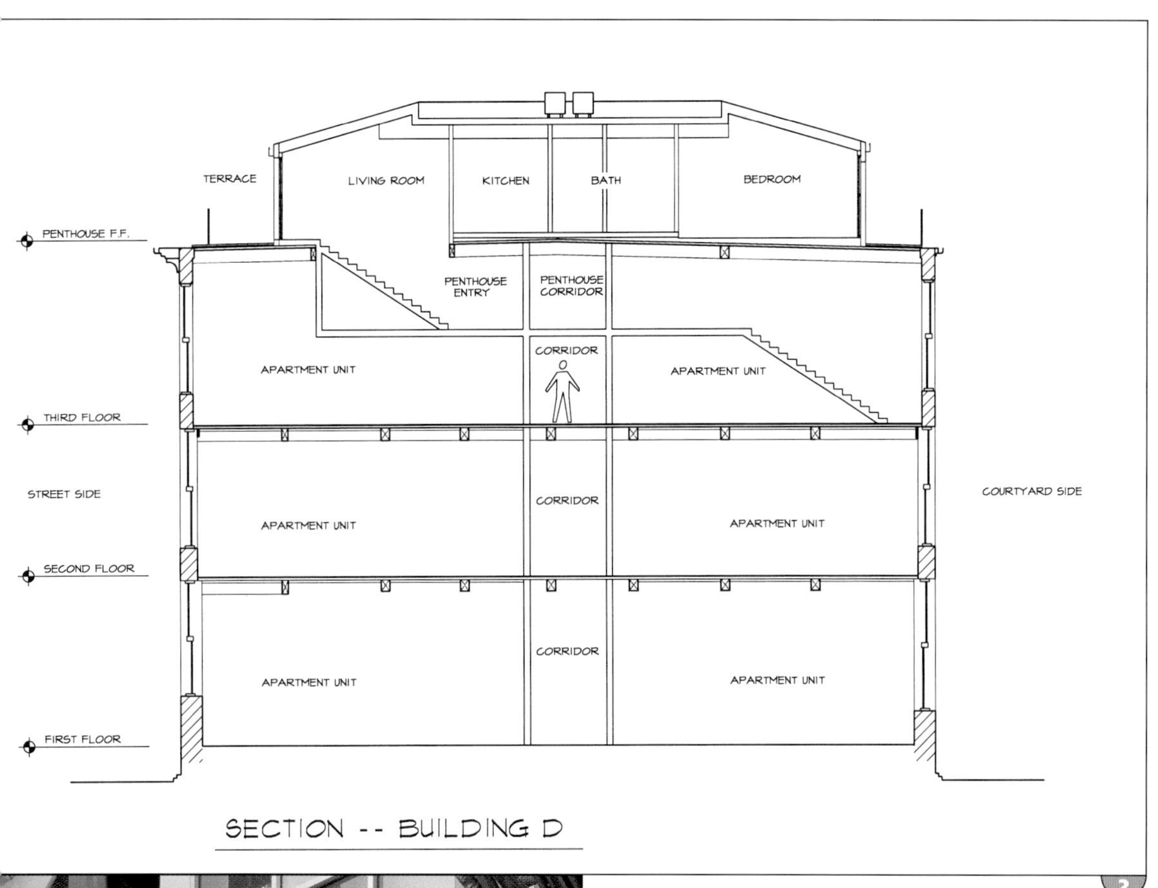

1

Once the largest cotton mill in the South, the original 1882 structure was rehabilitated to house 269 rental apartments and 18 condominium units.

2

Building section showing various unit configurations. Some units have double height ceilings; others are bilevel or loft units.

3

Building interiors blend old materials with new.

4

First floor plan.

5

Industrial equipment and materials were salvaged and used to create sculpture, now located throughout the project.

6

Of the original structure, as much as possible was retained. Cypress-framed windows were removed, refurbished, and replaced. Where possible, the wood strip flooring was retained.

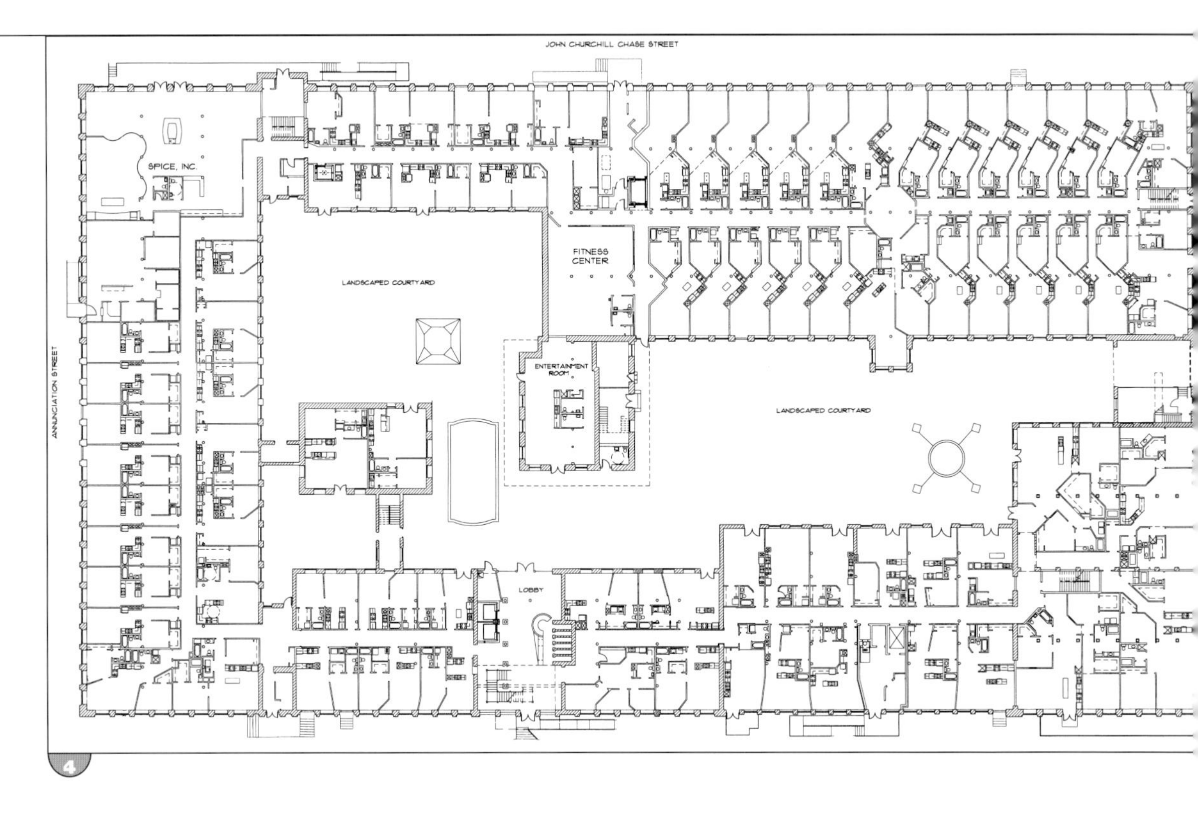

While some peripheral structures were removed to open up the courtyard, several other structures that contribute to the mill's historic identity were retained. The largest of these, the mill's water tower, was stripped of its lead paint and emblazoned with the Cotton Mill name. It is visible for miles around. In addition to its marketing value, the water tower serves as a telecommunications station and is leased to a local cellular service. Also retained were the mill's bell tower and a 120-foot-high, cylindrical brick boiler stack.

Taking its preservation philosophy a step further, HRI also sponsored an archeological survey of the site and funded a "Salvage/Object Art Initiative," for which local artist Paul Fowler took remnants of the mill's infrastructure—old boiler pipes, flues, and the like—and turned them into site sculpture.

Renovation of the Cotton Mill included cleaning and repairing of the mill's extensive brickwork. The brick was pressure-washed on both exterior and interior. Water containment systems were used on the interior to avoid damaging the wood floors. Much of the interior side of the brickwork had retained the100-year-old paint. Some of the paint was failing, and much of it was lead-based, which now must be treated as a hazardous material. The pressure wash was designed to remove only the unsound paint; well-adhered paint—whatever its aesthetic condition—was left in place as a reminder of the mill's industrial past. In accordance with federal Department of

5

Housing and Urban Development (HUD) requirements, however, all lead-based paint surfaces were repainted up to a height of 48 inches above the floor with a special lead-encapsulating paint. The result, by HRI's intention, is that the gritty history of the Cotton Mill remains intact, a feature that seems to appeal to the young, urban crowd that has leased the Cotton Mill apartments.

To comply with National Park Service standards for historic preservation, the 1,200-plus cypress windows were refurbished and reused. The monumental windows were removed from their frames and shipped out of state for chemical paint stripping. A workshop with nine workstations was established on site to

6

7

repair and reinstall the windows as they returned from stripping. On most windows, the upper sash was fixed in place and sealed to conserve energy—and minimize tenants' utility bills—while the lower sash was made operable. The stripped windows were left unpainted on the interior side.

Similarly, the wood strip flooring of the mill was retained in most cases. After the existing building interiors were gutted, the acres of remaining wood flooring were sanded down and coated with urethane for protection. Where the wood flooring could not be saved, the floors were either infilled with plywood panels or fitted with color-stained concrete slabs. Although the plywood was intended as a subflooring for carpeting, the decision was later made to clear-coat the plywood and use it as a finished floor, in keeping with the industrial ambience of the Cotton Mill.

The rooftop condominiums provided additional challenges. Although the building's original structural capacity allowed for construction on the roof without upgrading its foundations, it did require the localized reinforcement of columns and beams as well as construction of additional support beams. The bigger issue, though, was how to integrate the new construction with the old in terms of design and historic preservation, and how to screen off the required air conditioning units that were to be mounted on the roof.

These were more than aesthetic issues. Approval of the project's historic tax credits—the financial linchpin of the project—was contingent on approval by the state historic preservation office and the National Park Service. Months of design studies and site-line studies—even a full-size mock-up on the roof—were required to come to agreement on the massing of the rooftop construction. A related issue was the materials to be used for the facades of the condominium units. Aluminum panel construction was selected. Brick was not permitted by the Park Service because it would imitate the historic original, and stucco was judged to be too expensive and hard to maintain. As for the visibility of the air conditioning units, the solution was to set the units in a specially built trough within the volume of the condominium roofline, separated from the condominiums with several inches of sound-deadening concrete.

7, 8

An interior courtyard was rehabilitated to become a series of landscaped areas that now includes a pool. The original water tower and smokestack remain.

9

Original brickwork and timber beams imbue the development with a gritty industrial character, which was enhanced with such elements as concrete flooring, steel staircases, and new exposed ductwork.

The renovation and buildout of the Cotton Mill apartments were phased because of the large size of the project. Initially, two phases were planned, corresponding to the major building fire wall demarcations. Construction was staged "like a GM production line," notes Gary Meadows, president of HCI Construction and Design (HRI's in-house construction and architectural division), "with crews of each trade cycling through the buildings." Eventually, based on the evident market demand for the apartments, the project was divided into three phases, so that portions of the building could be occupied sooner than originally planned. The first tenants moved in 12 months after construction began. Construction was completed, except for some of the rooftop condominium work, in 18 months.

Given the constraints of working within the envelope of six different buildings—each with its own floor plate configuration—more than 30 different unit plans were required. Most of the apartments have a luxurious 12-foot ceiling height, and some top floor units have partial 20-foot-high ceilings. To further accentuate the historic character of the Cotton Mill, the mill's heavy timber structural columns have been exposed within the apartment units and hallways, rather than buried in drywall partitions. Similarly, the timber beams and metal tie rods have been left exposed, for both economy and visual interest.

To maintain a sense of openness, some interior partitions were built only eight feet high. Most kitchens are open to the adjacent space, and all units have side-by-side or stacked washer/dryer units. Each dwelling unit also has two telephone lines, with CAT5 cable for high-speed Internet access, as well as standard cable for TV.

10

The end product retains much of the original structure.

11

As is true in many industrial reuse projects, ceiling heights at the Cotton Mill are luxuriously high, ranging from 12 to 20 feet.

12

A major amenity is Spice, Inc., a gourmet food and carry-out shop that maintains the industrial look of the project.

Project amenities include the pool, courtyard, game room, and 1,500-square-foot fitness center. A full-time concierge is stationed in the main lobby.

One corner of the ground floor is occupied by Spice, Inc., a gourmet food and take-out shop, owned and operated by Susan Spicer, one of New Orleans's premier chefs. Spice, Inc., which also offers on-site cooking lessons, is "an amenity for the tenants," notes Tom Crumley, vice president and project manager for HRI, "as valuable to the marketing and livability

12

of the project as the swimming pool and fitness center."

The rooftop condominium units, which average about 1,600 square feet, are single-loaded so that they have panoramic views in two directions. The units are reached from a mezzanine, newly constructed by HRI within the 20-foot-high volume of the mill's existing top floor. The units have hardwood floors and granite countertops, features that were originally offered as upgrades but were requested so often that the developer has gone back and retrofitted all the units to this standard.

The Cotton Mill project was developed through a partnership, with HRI as the general partner and AmerUs Mutual Life Insurance Company as the limited, tax-credit partner. AmerUs provided $6.5 million in equity through the purchase of the project's historic tax credits as well as the purchase of tax credits generated from the donation of a preservation easement for the Cotton Mill's facade. HRI provided an additional $3 million in equity financing. The remainder of the project's $32.2 million cost was financed through a first mortgage, insured through HUD's 221(d)4 loan program and sold to a pension fund such as Ginnie Mae securities.

The Cotton Mill restoration clearly struck a chord in New Orleans. The progress of the restoration, the archeological dig, and the art initiative were widely reported in the local press. The project was even featured on the cover of *New Orleans* magazine. Echoing this media response, and perhaps generated by it, leasing of the Cotton Mill apartments proceeded at twice the expected pace; 95 percent occupancy was reached in 12 months, a rate of more than 20 units per month. Coupled with the rapid absorption rate, the rents exceeded the project's pro forma expectations by over 7 percent. Condominium sales have proceeded less rapidly, but generally have met pro forma expectations. With base prices ranging from $235,000 to $384,000, 14 of the 18 condominium units have been sold as of April 1999, averaging two units per month. Base sales prices have exceeded the originally budgeted prices by approximately 10 percent.

The Cotton Mill has taken a building of little economic use—one whose emptiness and deterioration could be expected to contribute to the disintegration of its inner-city neighborhood—and has used it as a vehicle to regenerate the neighborhood. Not only has a chapter of New Orleans's history been preserved, but also a neighborhood has been strengthened in the process. More specifically, the industrial character of the Cotton Mill has been particularly appealing to young New Orleans residents, and the developer has made a conscious effort to retain this aesthetic in the renovation process. The Salvage/Object Art Initiative sponsored by HRI has reinforced this aesthetic while at the same time serving as a bridge to the New Orleans arts community that has pioneered the Warehouse District revitalization.

case study

The Cotton Mill

New Orleans, Louisiana

land use information

Site Area:	2.836 acres, covering an entire city block
Total Dwelling Units:	287
Gross Building Area:	323,333 square feet
Gross Leasable Area:	253,408 square feet
Gross Project Density:	101 units per acre
Parking, Total:	190 off-site spaces
Parking Ratio:	0.66 space/unit
Project Completion Date:	April 1, 1999

land use plan

	Acres	**Percentage of Site**
Residential	1.916	68%
Recreation/Amenities	0.69	24% interior courtyard
Open Space	0.23	8% exterior green space
Total	2.836	100%

13
The water tower is a recognizable landmark that identifies the Cotton Mill and also brings additional revenue. It has been leased to a cellular telephone service for use as a communications tower.

development costs

	Total	Cost per Dwelling Unit	Cost per Residential Square Foot
Site Acquisition Cost	$3,513,000	$12,240	$10.86
Site Improvement Cost	$500,000	$1,742	$1.55
Construction Cost	$20,358,000	$70,933	$62.96
Soft Costs	$7,839,000	$27,313	$24.24
Total Development Cost	$32,210,000	$112,228	$99.62

unit information

Unit Type	Floor Area (Square Feet)	Number	Current Rent/ Sales Prices
Efficiency	639	27	$722
1-bdrm/1-bath	580	82	$655
1-bdrm/1-bath	670	35	$757
1-bdrm/1-bath	735	28	$831
1-bdrm/1-bath	939	15	$1,050
1-bdrm/1-bath lofts	1,515	2	$1,712
2-bdrm/2-bath lofts	984	66	$1,112
3-bdrm/2-bath lofts	1,551	14	$1,753
Rooftop condominiums	1,545	18	$235,000–$384,250
Total		287	

contact information

Developer	Historic Restoration, Inc. 210 Baronne Street, Suite 1717 New Orleans, Louisiana 70112 504-566-0204
Architect	HRI Group 210 Baronne Street, Suite 210 New Orleans, Louisiana 70112 504-679-5040
Contractor	HCI Construction & Design 210 Baronne Street, Suite 210 New Orleans, Louisiana 70112 504-679-5040

case study

site 17

seattle, washington

Site 17 does not look like its neighbors and that's just the point. The eight-story apartment building, located near downtown Seattle, is sheathed in bright yellow, red, and blue stucco and siding, alternating with galvanized, corrugated sheet metal. The building's "edginess," as architect Bill Gaylord of GGLO characterizes it, was inspired by the project's location in Belltown, Seattle's emerging arts district, and was designed to appeal to Seattle's younger and more artistically inclined population.

The "not-your-father's apartment" attitude carries over to the interior of the 97-unit building as well. Sixteen of the units are loft designs, common to San Francisco and other big cities, but relatively new to Seattle. "No one else was renting units with concrete floors," notes Tim Abell, project manager for

Note: Images for this case study are courtesy of Eduardo Calderon.

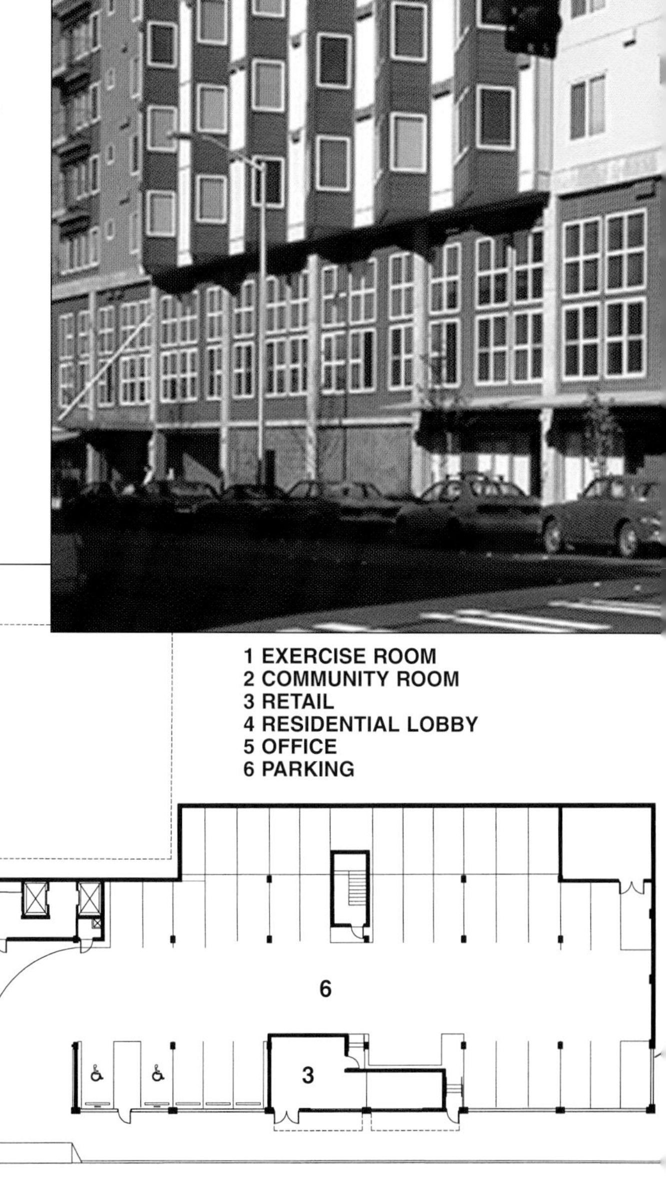

developer Harbor Properties, Inc. Metal artwork by local artist Kevin Spitzer, which lines the ground-floor facade, as well as a rooftop beacon, completes the aesthetic features, which resonate strongly in this warehouse/artist neighborhood.

Site 17 is built on a sloping half-acre site adjacent to a freeway ramp and an assortment of older industrial structures and newer residential buildings. The project is constructed over and around a three-level parking garage, which—because of the topography—can be entered at all three levels.

The eight-level building (six stories plus basement and mezzanine) reads as several smaller structures built on top of a three-story podium. A café is strategically located adjacent to the apartment lobby on the ground floor. Additional storefront space is interspersed along the principal elevation, in between the artist-designed grillwork that screens the parking area. Filling out the remainder of the concrete podium are the two-story loft apartments, with large, square picture windows over the street. A sheltered courtyard sits on the roof of the podium, shielded by the five-story, wood-framed apartment blocks.

1
First level plan.

2, 3
Site 17 is built as a five-level wood-frame structure over a three-level concrete base. The base contains the lobby and retail spaces, parking, and two-story loft units. A variety of materials, colors, and forms breaks the massing of the block-long structure into smaller components, yielding a rich visual palette that appeals to the project's young urban target market.

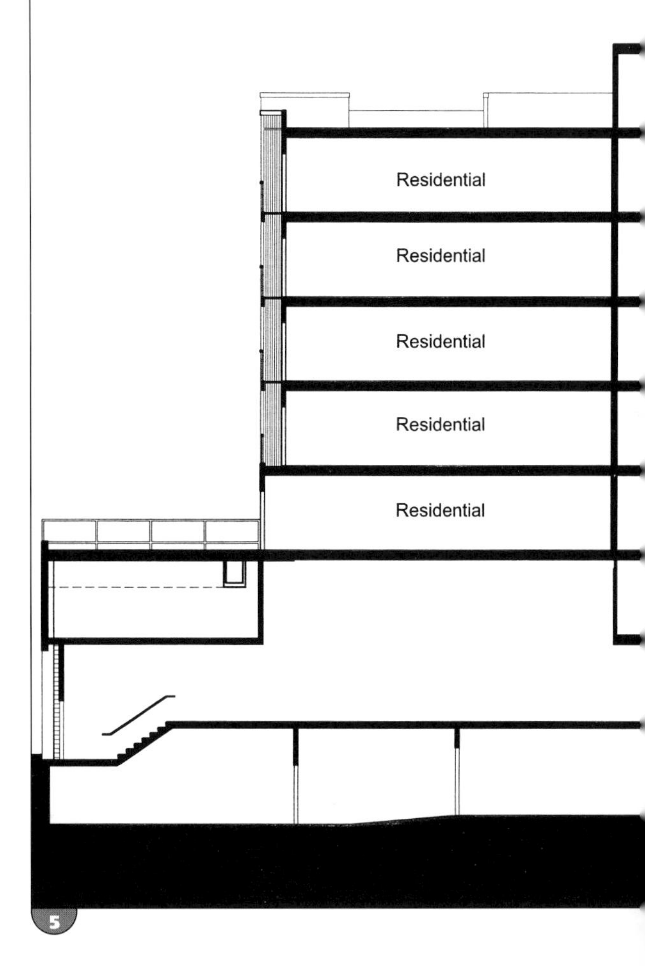

The varied massing of the building has both prosaic and poetic roots. Fundamentally, the massing is a response to the property's zoning envelope, which required a 25-foot view corridor through the site for each 125 feet of wall length. Metaphorically, the designers took the zoning mandate as a means to create a "village": a group of facades appearing to have grown up out of the site, one at a time, similar to the organic growth of the city. To this end, the facades have been broken up into a series of color planes, advancing and receding, modulated by balcony and bay window attachments.

On the interior, the industrial aesthetic is most pronounced in the loft apartments. Mechanical ducts and plumbing lines have been left exposed in both the hallways and within the loft dwelling units. Floors are bare concrete; doors, trim work, and cabinets are made of clear-finished MDF (medium-density fiberboard)—a wood product that is usually painted. Door frames are clear-coated raw steel, and stairs and railings are constructed of galvanized steel and checkerplate. Appliances are "black-on-black," and kitchen bar counters are made of terrazzo with embedded recycled glass chips.

In the remainder of the project—the studios and the one- and two-bedroom units—the finishes are less raw, although still a step beyond developer beige. Apartment units are carpeted and have standard drywall ceilings. Some have MDF detailing similar to the loft units.

The dwelling unit mix favors smaller units, in order to keep the units affordable to the young target market. About one-third of the units are studios (580 to 650 square feet) and another third are one-bedroom units (600 to 650 square feet). The loft units vary in size, from 720 to 990 square feet. Sixteen of the project's 97 dwelling units have two bedrooms and range in size from 1,050 to 1,200 square feet.

The live/work loft units have 17-foot-high ceilings, while the flats have ceilings eight feet high. Along with the usual kitchen appliances, all apartments have washers and dryers. And, in a bow to their high-tech setting, the dwelling units are wired with CAT5 cable for high-speed Internet access. Ten percent of

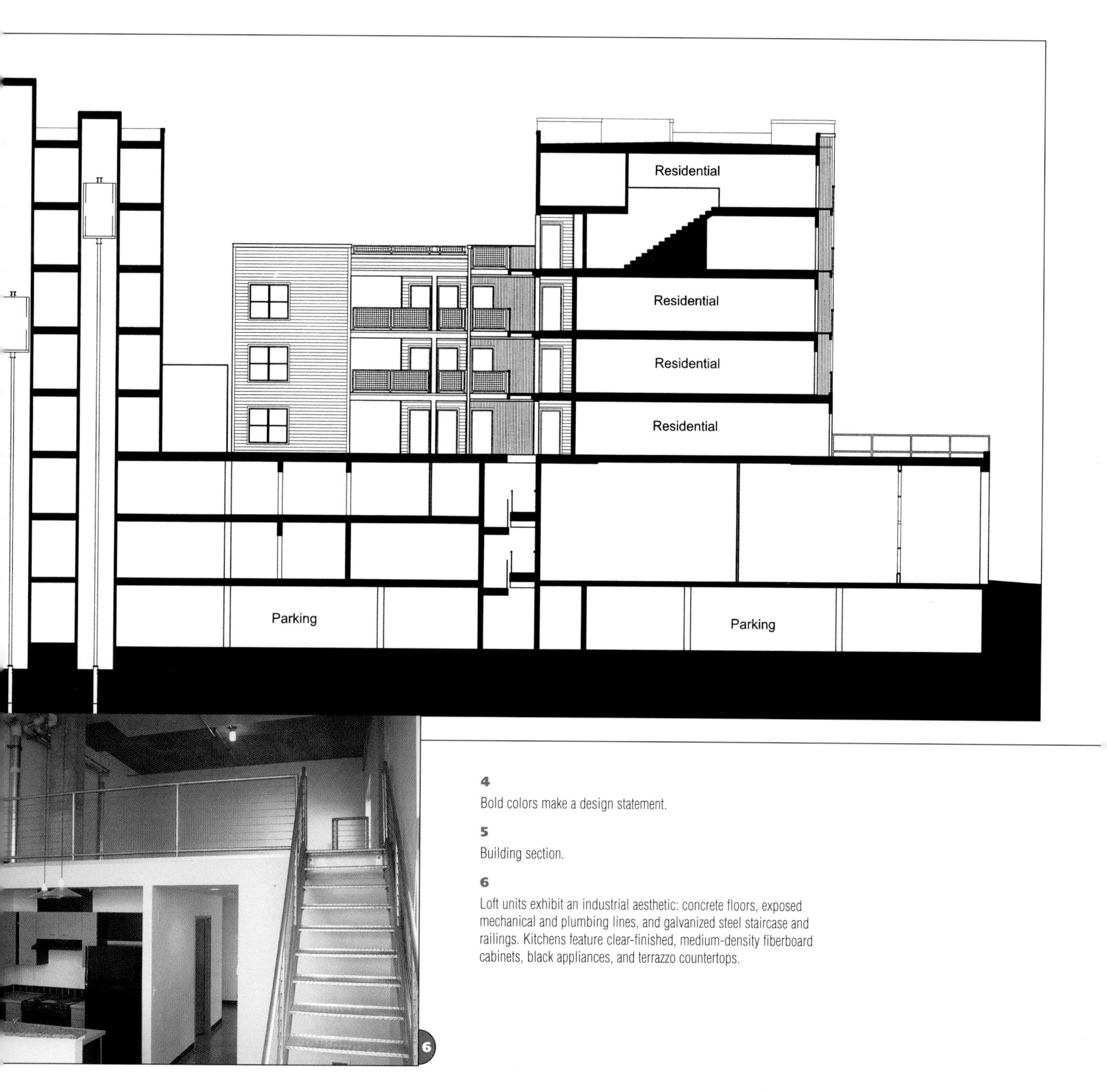

4

Bold colors make a design statement.

5

Building section.

6

Loft units exhibit an industrial aesthetic: concrete floors, exposed mechanical and plumbing lines, and galvanized steel staircase and railings. Kitchens feature clear-finished, medium-density fiberboard cabinets, black appliances, and terrazzo countertops.

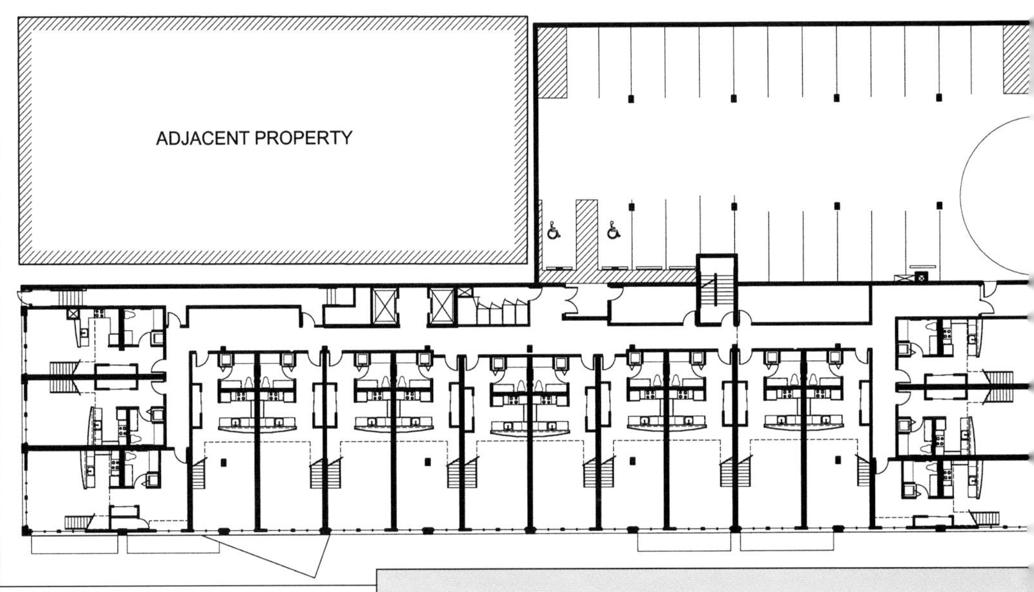

7

In the lobby, industrial materials combine with warm colors and textures.

8

Second level plan.

9

View of building from interior courtyard.

10

An artist designed the metal grillwork that shields the parking garage. The pattern represents the building's site plan and location map.

the dwelling units are fully accessible to the disabled, and the remainder are adaptable. Project amenities include the fourth-floor courtyard plus a deck on the seventh-floor roof. A community room and an exercise room are located adjacent to the ground-floor lobby.

Given the L shape of the site, most of the apartments are single-loaded along a corridor. Above the parking podium, the corridors are mostly exterior, unconditioned spaces, ringing the courtyard. Although the weather is sometimes harsh in Seattle, keeping the corridors open meant that the they do not have to be fire-rated, which allowed the architects to locate bedrooms with windows against the corridor.

Construction of Site 17 took about 13 months. The biggest difficulty was finding enough rough framers to build five stories of wood framing. Marketing began, according to developer Tim Abell of Harbor Properties, almost from the first day of construction. The marketing effort was aided in no small part by the project's visibility from the adjacent freeway ramp. The sales pitch was as clear as the view: "Lofts and apartments with attitude," proclaimed the project's brochure.

By opening day, 80 percent of the units had been rented, and full occupancy was achieved just three months later. While Abell confesses, in retrospect, to having experienced some degree of "nervousness" regarding the untested and relatively raw loft units, the live/work units proved to be very popular. "The demand just isn't being met by stucco boxes," he notes. Overall, the strongest demand was for the most affordable units (at the bottom of the project) and for the best units with the best views (at the top).

Site 17 has been so successful that Harbor Properties is embarking on a companion building across the street. And based on the market reaction to Site 17's architectural "attitude," the new version is "going to be more edgy and bold," says Abell, with more raw spaces and more color in the apartments. The new building will have fewer large units, however, based on the absorption experience of the first phase.

The developer's decision to open the building up to the neighborhood—by including ground-floor commercial spaces and artist-designed street furniture—has proven successful. However, Abell believes that more retail space could have been absorbed. In the upcoming phase of the project, he intends to provide additional ground-floor commercial space, which will be of benefit to both buildings.

9

10

case study

site 17

seattle, washington

land use information

Site Area:	0.5 acre
Total Dwelling Units:	97
Gross Project Density:	194 units per acre
Housing Type:	Rental apartments
Gross Residential Density:	202 units per acre
Parking, Total:	83 spaces
Parking Ratio:	0.86 space/unit
Project Completion Date:	September 1998 (Phase I)

land use plan

	Acres	Percentage of Site
Residential	0.48[1]	96%[1]
Open Space	0.02	4%
Total	0.50	100%

[1]Includes parking and amenities.

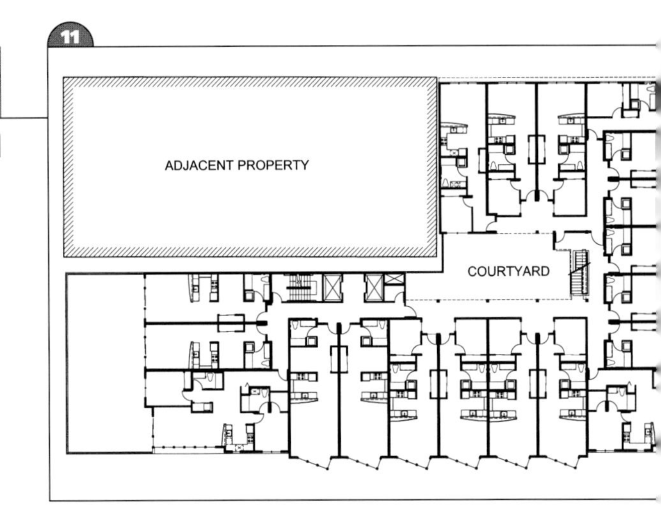

contact information

Developer	Harbor Properties, Inc. 500 Union Street Suite 200 Seattle, Washington 98101 206-623-0916
Architect	GGLO Architecture and Interior Design 1191 Second Avenue Suite 1650 Seattle, Washington 98101 206-467-5828
Artist	Kevin Spitzer D.K. Studios 2942 Southwest Avalon Seattle, Washington 98126 206-935-5351

development costs

	Total	Cost per Dwelling Unit	Cost per Residential Square Foot
Site Acquisition Cost	$1,600,000[2]	$16,495	$16.32
Site Improvement Cost	N/A	N/A	N/A
Construction Cost	$6,400,000	$65,979	$65.29
Soft Costs	$2,500,000	$25,773	$25.50
Total Development Cost	$10,500,000	$108,247	$107.11

[2] Appraisal value.

unit information

Unit Type	Floor Area (Square Feet)	Number of Units	Current Rent
Artist loft	720–990	16	$1,200–$1,600
Studio	580–650	35	$800–$1,200
1-bdrm	600–650	30	$800–$1,200
2-bdrm	1,050–1,200	16	$1,650–$1,700
Total		97	

11
Fourth level showing interior courtyard.

12
The courtyard serves both as a circulation spine and as private outdoor space for residents. Access to some units is via exterior walkways.

13
Detail.

14
First-floor storefronts are shielded with corrugated aluminum awnings.

case study

The Exchange

New York, New York

The Exchange is a 21-story high-rise building located one block south of the New York Stock Exchange in the skyscraper canyons of lower Manhattan. Constructed as an office building in 1899, the imposing Italianate-style structure was one of New York City's earliest steel-frame skyscrapers. After a century of service, however, little demand remained for its now-antiquated office space, and the interior of the building was gutted in 1996 and reconstructed as 345 rental apartments.

In the early 1990s, the national economy was in the midst of a slump, and Wall Street was experiencing a major decline. By 1994, office buildings in the financial district had vacancy rates as high as 30 percent, leaving some 25 million square feet of space unoccupied. Much of this space, like that of the Exchange, had become obsolete, needing major renovations to attract new office tenants, even if demand were to improve. In the midst of this office space glut, however, residential vacancies citywide had remained extremely low, with rents averaging about $2.50 per square foot per month.

In 1996, with Wall Street in apparent free fall, the city of New York formulated the Lower Manhattan Revitalization Plan, which included a tax incentive package to encourage residential conversions in the financial district. This was a rare case in which city government, preservationists, and developers all shared a common goal: to stem the decline of the financial district and its architectural patrimony. The solution, acknowledged by all three sectors, was to encourage residential development in the district and to create more of a mixed-use, 24-hour community.

The tax component of the revitalization plan provided property tax exemptions and abatements in connection with conversion of nonresidential buildings to housing. For a building like the Exchange, the plan allows for 100 percent abatement of the property taxes that would accrue from the increased assessed value of the structure for the first nine years after the conversion. Partial, declining abatements are provided for four years thereafter. Further, the existing assessed taxable base is exempted from property taxes for ten years, also with partial, declining exemptions in the subsequent four years.

In addition to the tax incentives, the city took other steps to facilitate residential development. It eliminated zoning restrictions that had effectively precluded residential conversions and formed the Alliance for Downtown New York, a business/government partnership that administers a downtown business improvement district. The city has also worked to improve public services, such as street cleaning and trash removal.

The developer, Crescent Heights, purchased the Exchange—then known as 25 Broad Street—in October 1994, before the city's tax

1

Note: Images for this case study are courtesy of Crescent Heights Development.

1, 2

The craftsmanship of a bygone era has been preserved: the stately old structure at 21 Broad Street in lower Manhattan now houses 345 luxury rental apartments.

3
LR/DR
BR
MBR
LR
PUBLIC CORRIDOR
2BR
1407 SF
1BR
700 SF
LAUNDRY
COMMERCIAL LEASE SPACE #1
COMMERCIAL LEASE SPACE #2
COMMERCIAL LEASE SPACE #3
EXCHANGE PLACE LOBBY
BROAD STREET LOBBY
MULTI-PURPOSE ROOM

3

Typical floor plan. Below: street-level floor plan.

4

Carved limestone garlands grace the refurbished windows of the lower floors. Upper-floor windows were replaced with more energy-efficient units of the same style.

incentives came into effect. At about $10 per square foot, the property was so undervalued at that time, notes Bruce Menin of Crescent Heights, that "even storage space would have been an economically viable use for the property." Once the tax program was instituted, however, it was clear that the highest and best use of the structure would be rental housing. The tax incentives also made all the difference to lenders, who initially were reluctant to lend on what was then a pioneering and untested venture. The developer had been seeking financing for 18 months, but it was not until the tax incentive plan was in place that a lender, CS First Boston, agreed to finance the project. The result was the first large-scale construction loan in the financial district in many years.

Designed by the architectural firm of Clinton & Russell, 25 Broad Street was the most valuable building in New York at the time it was built. Intricate limestone garlands and other classical details adorn the stately facade of the Italianate building. Tall fluted columns flank the grand Broad Street entrance.

The original exterior features of the building have been preserved, for the most part, in the course of the renovation. The exterior stonework was cleaned, and the windows on the first four floors were renovated and repainted. Windows above the fourth floor were replaced with more energy-efficient windows that are similar in appearance.

Inside, the ornate, turn-of-the-century lobby has been restored. The original granite floors, dark wood paneling, and marble pilasters capped by gilded Corinthian capitals provide an opulent setting—the perfect image of luxury sought for the residences above. From the lobby, twin marble staircases take visitors to the second-floor leasing office.

The upper floors were totally gutted and rebuilt, with 16 dwelling units on each floor. New electrical, plumbing, and HVAC facilities were installed throughout. A new telecommunications system also was installed, providing high-speed Internet access to every apartment, along with a buildingwide intranet. Twelve of the 17 original elevators were removed to create additional floor area. The five remaining elevators were refurbished with new mahogany paneling. Two new fire stairs were built to comply with current code requirements.

Both the common areas and the apartments are generous in size because of the deep floorplates of the original office building. In the common areas, this deeper window-to-core distance has allowed for wide corridors and large elevator lobbies, substantial storage areas, and a laundry room on each floor (three-bedroom units have their own washers/dryers). One-bedroom units typically contain 800 square feet, compared with a market norm of about 650 square feet. Bathrooms are unusually large; most, have double sinks. Pocket doors close the tub area off from the remainder of the bathroom, which can serve as a powder room for guests. Most units have walk-in closets. Ceilings typically are about ten feet high, although some are as high as 16 feet.

"Space is the first luxury in housing," comments Costas Kondylis, renovation architect for the Exchange, and the deep floorplates and high floor-to-floor heights have turned necessity into a virtue. Given the lack of views in the canyons of Wall Street, and the lack of retail

5

and services in the area, space was the most potent amenity that developer Crescent Heights had to offer. That, and luxury appointments. In keeping with the spatial opulence, the developer provided a richer palette of finishes throughout the units, from parquet wood flooring to tall wood baseboard moldings to raised panel doors.

Similarly, the operating philosophy of the Exchange is to provide the service and amenities of a quality hotel. Amenities at the Exchange include valet and concierge services, a doorman (two at rush hour), two executive-quality conference rooms, an oversized gym, a video rental room, and a rooftop sundeck. As the pioneering project in the neighborhood, notes developer Menin, the building had to be clearly superior to the competition in order to bring residents into the newly developing neighborhood. Even as the neighborhood has become more established, however, it has remained important for the building to provide a first-rate offering, according to Menin, in order to remain competitive with new entries to the market.

The three retail spaces in the building are seen as strategically significant in this regard. One is being developed as an upscale market, café, and restaurant. A second space, at the basement level (with street-level access), contains a 7,500-square-foot space that was originally used for vault storage. The vaults remain and are expected to provide a unique design element for a catering facility and lounge. Planning options for the third retail space include a luxury spa that would serve as an amenity for both the building and the neighborhood.

Parking is not provided in the building, but for transit-comfortable New Yorkers, notes architect Kondylis, this has not been a significant impediment. Parking is available in nearby commercial garages for the 20 percent or so who keep a car in the city.

In planning for the Exchange, the developer expected the project to appeal to singles and couples who work in the financial district. Only about half of the residents of the Exchange fall into this category, however. The developer reports a surprising number of families, drawn to the building because of the large units and relative affordability compared with units of similar quality in uptown neighborhoods. The building also has drawn reverse commuters, attracted both to the features of the historic building and to city living.

Occupancy at the Exchange has remained near 100 percent since initial lease-up was achieved in 1997. Little advertising has been necessary, just standard newspaper promotion. The Exchange is one of the few rental apartment buildings in Manhattan that is 100 percent market rate and not subject to rent control.

6

At this point, the financial district is still in transition. Several office buildings have been converted to residential use since the Exchange was completed, although prices for potentially convertible office buildings have been rising, and demand for office space has bounced back, slowing the trend. New retail and service businesses have sprouted in concert with the residential development—but like the residential conversions, the new businesses have not reached a critical mass. The face of the financial district is gradually changing, however. New restaurants and services continue to set up shop in the neighborhood, an optimistic sign for the future of both the district and the city.

5

A pair of neoclassical marble staircases flank the main entrance and take visitors to the leasing office on the second floor.

6

Old buildings can be like buried treasures. Once the grime is scraped away, magnificent riches are revealed. In the lobby, the original granite, marble, mahogany, and gilt set a tone of luxury.

case study

the exchange

New York, New York

contact information

Developer	Crescent Heights Development 555 Northeast 15th Street Miami, Florida 33132 305-374-5700
Architect	Costas Kondylis & Associates, PC 3 West 18th Street New York, New York 10011 212-727-8688

land use information

Site Area:	0.57 acre
Total Dwelling Units:	345
Gross Project Density:	605 units per acre
Housing Type:	Rental apartments
Parking, Total:	none
Project Completion Date:	January 1998

unit information

Unit Type	Floor Area (Square Feet)	Number of Units	Current Rents
Studio	735–922	2	$2,000–$3,100
1-bdrm	683–1,042	177	$2,000–$4,200
2-bdrm	927–1,533	145	$2,500–$4,500
3-bdrm	2,554–2,931	21	$4,800–$10,000
Total		345	

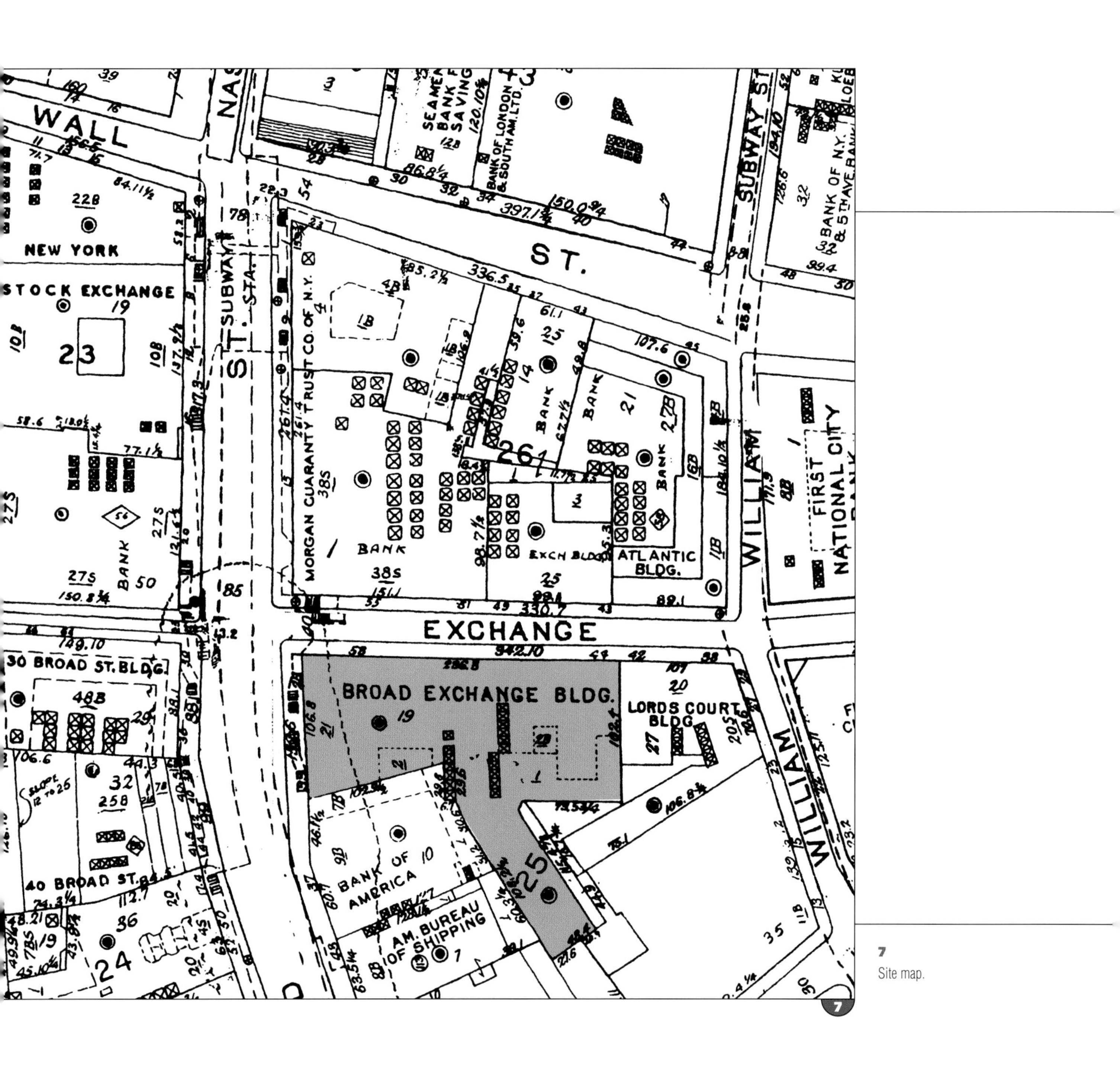
WALL
ST.
EXCHANGE
WILLIAM
SUBWAY ST.
SUBWAY
ST. STA.
NEW YORK
STOCK EXCHANGE
BANK
MORGAN GUARANTY TRUST CO. OF N.Y.
BANK
BANK
BANK
BANK
EXCH BLDG.
ATLANTIC BLDG.
BANK OF LONDON & SOUTH AM. LTD.
BANK OF N.Y. & 5TH AVE. BANK
FIRST NATIONAL CITY
30 BROAD ST. BLDG.
BROAD EXCHANGE BLDG.
LORDS COURT BLDG.
BANK OF AMERICA
40 BROAD ST.
AM. BUREAU OF SHIPPING
WILLIAM

7
Site map.

summary table

Project Name	Location	Type of Dwelling Unit (1) SFD	2–4/TH	MF	Number of Dwelling Units
Middleton Hills	Middleton, Wisconsin	●	●	●	635
Amberleigh	Mill Creek, Washington		●		88
Harbor Town	Memphis, Tennessee	●	●	●	875
Orenco Station	Hillsboro, Oregon	●	●	●	446[6]
Crawford Square	Pittsburgh, Pennsylvania	●	●	●	426
The Pointe at Lincoln Park	Chicago, Illinois		●		154
Metro Senior Housing & CityPark	Foster City, California		●	●	102
Addison Circle	Addison, Texas		●	●	3,000
Oriental Warehouse	San Francisco, California			●	66
Courthouse Hill	Arlington, Virginia		●	●	202
Paseo Plaza	San Jose, California		●	●	210
The Cotton Mill	New Orleans, Louisiana			●	287
Site 17	Seattle, Washington			●	97
The Exchange	New York, New York			●	345

Acreage	Density: Gross Project Density (2)	Density: Gross Residential Density (3)	Building Type (4): Low-Rise	Building Type (4): Mid-Rise	Building Type (4): High-Rise	Tenure (5)
160.0	4.0	6.3	●			S + R
15.2	5.8	7.6	●			S
135.0	6.5	9.6	●			S + R
61.2	7.3	10.8	●			S + R
24.0	17.8	18.4	●			S + R Assisted
7.0	21.7	23.6		●		S
3.6	28.0	44.3	●	●		S + R Assisted
80.0	37.5	54.6		●		R
1.5	44.4	63.5		●		S
4.6	43.9	69.7	●	●		S
2.9	73.4	137.3		●		R
2.8	101.0	149.8		●		R + S
0.5	194.0	202.0			●	R
0.6	605.0	605.0			●	R

Notes:

1 SFD= Single-family detached
2–4/TH = 2- to 4- unit structures and townhouses
MF = Multifamily

2 Total number of dwelling units divided by total project acreage

3 Total number of dwelling units divided by total residential acreage plus roads/parking acreage

4 Low-rise = 1 to 3 stories
Mid-rise = 4 to 6 stories
High-rise = 7 or more stories

5 S = For-sale housing
R = Rental housing

6 In sections built to date